# YOUR MORTAL EYES WILL SEE NO MORE

*Anna*

ISBN-13: 978-0692142332
ISBN-10: 0692142339

## DEDICATION

This book is dedicated to my wonderful mother, Esther Ruth Bazelides, who was kind, caring, and a best friend for life.

# CHAPTER ONE

Jeff watched the crowd as he stood by the bar in a stunning tuxedo. He had been invited to a royal wedding and had been looking forward to the event for months. The banquet hall was enchanting with golden chandeliers and doorknobs, and large bouquets with many different types of lovely flowers were placed generously around the room so that a beautiful fragrance filled the air wherever there was movement. A long banquet table was set awaiting the wedding party with the bridegroom's place at the head of the table.

The orchestra was hidden behind a sheer drape that was sapphire in color. Music had been floating through the hall, and as the evening progressed, the musicians began to play a waltz so that the elegantly dressed couples would slowly stroll out on the ballroom floor. As the pairs swirled around the room, the scene was as if dozens of brightly colored butterflies were fluttering around the grand span.

He had never seen an event so charmingly planned, and as Jeff walked around the room smiling and saying hello to people, he came upon the fabulous food laden tables set out for all to enjoy until the grand dinner. He was hungry, so he decided to visit the buffet where he chose a lovely piece of bread. Leisurely, Jeff took a bite of the exotic food, and as he turned from the table, two very large men appeared in front of him. Both were finely dressed, but it was extremely plain they were not there as guests of the party. They both wore a very serious expression, and as the visitor smiled at them, they gave no indication of being friendly.

Suddenly, the one on the left grabbed Jeff's arm and told the other man to take his right. He asked them what they were doing as he struggled to free himself. Neither answered, and no one in the room acted as if there was a problem. "Throw him out into the dark; he doesn't belong in here," the man giving the orders said.

1

Jeff began to resist even harder, so one lifted him by the arms and the other took his feet and carried him to the front door. "I don't know how you got in, but you don't deserve to be here," and the man nodded to the other to toss Jeff out. He landed hard on the cement outside, and the entrance door shut with the sound of a judgement being final.

Slowly, Jeff stood up feeling as if his arm and hip bones had been broken. After a minute, he regained his composure a bit and turned slightly to the left noticing that it was so dark around him he couldn't see his hand in front of his face.

He thought about going back into the party and demand to know why he had been ushered out. The unwelcomed guest began dusting off his tuxedo and smoothing his hair back. He was as prominent as anyone at the party and actually had felt superior to most. How dare they treat him as if he wasn't a member of that level of society. Perhaps they just didn't know who he was.

Unexpectedly, a low growl was heard very close in the black environment. The pitch of the vibration increased to a snarl that was mixed with hissing. Jeff peered around but could see nothing. He stood very still afraid that any movement would cause him to touch what was being heard. In the next eerie instant breath could be felt on the side of his face, and as his eyes adjusted to the darkness, blood shot eyes were looking into his. He let out a hysterical scream as the monstrous shadow pushed closer to him.

"Did you really think you would be allowed to stay in there?" the thing asked. "You will never be let into that banquet again, so you might as well get used to us. But in time you will not be interested in that type of function. You want the same things we do, and we care about no one or nothing except gaining what we want."

Jeff's eyes spanned the area around him allowing a view of the entire thing that had spoken. He stepped back from the creature, but the thing just stepped closer to him and started to speak again. "Don't be afraid. We are always around, but you never see us. Most don't believe we really exist or don't care."

The stunned man stood there with his mouth wide open staring at the scariest being he had ever seen. The thing had the shape of a human, but the head was formed oddly and sitting on the body without a neck. Its mouth was twisted down and wrapped around the head part way and there were gashes in its skin all over the face that looked like someone or something had dug and clawed at it. The thing had one very large eye and one that was very small, and even though it was freely doing as it pleased, the eyes showed hopelessness and apathy. Its top lip looked as if it had been twisted out of shape, and it had sores all over the top lip that stuck out like a snout over its chin. There were lesions dotting its body everywhere seeping puss that made the air foul. More beasts like it were standing all around. Some were taller, some thinner, some standing more crooked or looking more hideous than the first.

The creature that had been speaking continued with a sarcastic tone, "I am Hamartolos, and I have been sent to let you know we are waiting for you. You can call on us anytime to assist you with all of your desires. We help to make decisions so you thoroughly enjoy your life on this earth and do everything you want to. After all," he leaned forward, "it is your life, and you should decide to have things that will give you as much pleasure and comfort as you want. Others are not a consideration." The beast smirked wickedly.

All of the other creatures around moved closer to the frightened human and one started to rub his arm. Jeff began to shake hard not knowing what to do, so he started to stumble through the dark. Finally falling down, he lay on the ground groaning.

Hamartolos stood above him, "You cannot escape! You are ours, so it is just a matter of time. We patiently wait to tear at your skin and take your selfish will to the depths of despair!!!!" Hamartolos swore at the others as they all disappeared. Jeff lay on the ground unable to move. He didn't know what to do, so he called for help. No one responded.

Opening his eyes, the dreamer sat straight up in his bed. Wringing with sweat, he looked around the room quickly to see if the beasts were lurking. He instinctively looked over at Emily to see if she had experienced the same thing, but she was sleeping soundly. He sat back realizing it had been a nightmare and he was in his own house and bedroom. Taking a deep breath, he rested his head against the headboard while listening to his heart pound hard. Sitting there for some time, the pounding pulse finally started to quiet down. "What a nightmare. I wonder what brought that on and what all those things were."

Carefully standing up and waiting until his legs felt steady, he went into the bathroom to take some aspirin. His head hurt and his body ached, so Jeff sat on the edge of the tub and put the pills in his mouth before drinking the entire glass of water. The shaking wouldn't stop and the questions of why such a bad dream like that would occur and what the meaning of such an awful vision would be whirled in his mind.

After the shock had worn off, an analysis of the dream and all that had happened began. He hadn't caused any trouble anywhere, so why would he be thrown out of a party. Not recognizing anyone in the dream, he wondered where the creatures had come from. Maybe they had been seen in a horror movie or something and were just not remembered.

Trying to figure out why his subconscious was spawning such ideas and dramatic images, his everyday actions and decisions were reviewed for a possible clue. Almost everything he had done for quite a while concerned the business, so an examination of the dealings taken for the company came to mind. He knew that some deeds were not accomplished with the greatest of integrity and morals.

Immediately, an inner voice began to justify his behavior over the last several years, "I have been working so hard to help others. All I have done is work to improve the world, and sometimes I had to take a few steps around the straight path in order to accomplish the goal. I didn't hurt anyone, and in the long run, everyone will benefit. Stretching the truth to get what I need and want to reach my objectives can't be wrong. The dream was from just being too tired, so it really just needs to be forgotten." He nodded to himself in what was believed to be a sensible reason for the nightmare.

Being a pillar of society, he would never be excluded or treated like that in the real world. Then he thought of the thing called Hamartolos, and he remembered what the beast said about Jeff being like them. "Ridiculous," he thought, but for just a second there was a feeling deep inside that told him he was wrong and was acting without standards and scruples. "Ridiculous," he thought again and brushed the thought from his mind.

# CHAPTER TWO

Looking at the clock, he saw that it was only three in the morning. There was no interest in going back to sleep, and his attention flowed to some work that had been put off. Down the stairs in the study the new manual that had just been printed was laying on the desk, so he quickly retrieved the handbook and became absorbed in reviewing the pages. The new material had to impress organizations that were potential funding sources for the educational research, development, and publishing company that he had started.

The research focused on scholastic topics, student development tactics, and how education could be changed to allow students to comprehend more quickly and retain the information longer. The avenues that would be used to disperse all educational tools included cyber, print, video, and audio that was applicable to the area being served, and of course, in different languages as expansion took place. Once the techniques were tested and approved, they were loaded on-line or published for use.

The current technological research was being watched as well, and Jeff believed that in a few years instruction could be added that would be loaded into a robot that was able to instruct students. As futuristic devices began to take over the classroom, the focus would turn mostly to this type of production. Over time, the expansion of the new technology into worldwide markets would increase the demand for his products.

He had started the enterprise three years earlier with a few large companies agreeing to back his work. As the investigation into the processes grew, he knew that more business people would have to be targeted to increase funding. So far, his company had accomplished some of what he wanted to do but there was a long way to go. The key concept that would bring in the capital needed to advance his research, development, and publishing services was to show businesses how they would benefit most from the educated and ambitious young who came in search of jobs. Another selling point would be access to all of the information the corporations supporting his business would have. Through his business, companies could learn of national, regional, and local schools, community colleges, and universities that utilized the techniques of the published products giving them first chance of employing outstanding workers.

From the calculations made as the structure of the business progressed, Jeff believed he would certainly be able to fund his organization fully by getting a few more large corporations as donors. As contacts from different parts of the country increased, the opportunity to expand his organization would grow dramatically.

Most CEOs were upstanding citizens and would have to be handled with care, but there were a few who would assist him by capitalizing on the success of the business for their own benefit and insist on first picks from the exceptional students educated with the new training available.

Of course Jeff knew that the country's smartest entrepreneurs were what guided national economic success, and the new training techniques would produce many more industrialists, but that was not his first priority. His first concern was himself and creating the type of life that he wanted. He had come from a poor family and did not intend to spend any more days in poverty. If CEOs needed to be catered to, then they would be accommodated.

Looking at his watch, he couldn't believe it was already nine a.m. The phone rang just as the last line of the new proposal for one of the CEOs he would meet with that morning was being written. The number showing on the screen told him that it was his fiancée, so he answered. "Hi sweetie," Emily said. "I just wanted to remind you that we are to meet at the church at seven tonight to discuss our wedding plans and set a date. I didn't tell you this morning on my way out because you looked so busy I didn't want to bother you. I am so excited and want to move the date up if we can get the church earlier!" She didn't hear a response, so she said, "Jeff?"

"Yeah, I'm here. I'll try to be there, but I have meetings all day, and they are very important appointments. I'll do everything I can to get there." This time, he heard silence. "Baby you know I want to get this settled as much as you do. I have to ensure our future as well. If I am late, work with Fr. Lore and I will get with you about the details. I love you, and I will see you later. Oh, remind me to tell you about the crazy nightmare I had last night." He hung up and shook his head. He loved Emily, but sometimes she pushed too hard and didn't prioritize like she should. Well, she would have to change once they finally got married.

Jeff looked at the document he had created one more time and then sprinted up the stairs to take a shower. His first meeting was in one hour, and he couldn't be late. He would be discussing the proposal with Ms. Etonly, and she would be tough to convince. Emphasis would have to be put on the children and their needs, and he would have to dodge the questions about the business' books. If this one found out what his salary was each year and the perks that came along with his position, she would never agree.

"I'll take her to the site and let her talk to the researchers," he decided. "She can walk around and see the different projects being worked, and that should satisfy her for the time being. I can tell her we will discuss the debits and credits on our balance sheet when all of the contributors meet."

## CHAPTER THREE

As he stepped outside, he noticed what a beautiful day it was in Orlando. The azure sky showed no signs of clouds, and the high temperature was forecast at around eighty-two degrees. This was the time of year that Jeff loved to go to the beach. He shook his head knowing there would not be time for the seashore for quite a while.

Orlando was a perfect place for his company. There were many corporate headquarters in the area, and there were many different types of schools he could work with to find out what was currently being done for the students. The higher class private schools, the public schools in different areas that shouldered different needs, the charter schools, as well as the juvenile detention homes that required training assistance were all there for him to investigate and work with. The same held true for every corner of the world, and Jeff had decided some time ago that he would expand his business across the nation as soon as the site he was running was solidly funded and the right contacts were made. Eventually, they could go worldwide, and the prospects of meeting needs around the globe were endless.

Jeff pulled into the parking garage at the Sun Dialee Insurance Headquarters where Ms. Etonly was the CEO. Having visited here before, the receptionist remembered him. "Hello Mr. Bellows," she said with a smile. "Ms. Etonly is in another meeting, but you can wait in her office." Jeff smiled and followed the redheaded assistant into the plush executive's domain and to a very expensive and comfortable chair. "Could I get you something to drink?" she asked. He shook his head no and watched her leave the room. As soon as she was gone, he started to scan the contents of the office.

"There it is," he thought, "a picture of Sarah." Memories flooded into his mind about the woman he had once hoped to marry.

She was Ms. Etonly's niece, and thankfully, the CEO had never known that her niece had been part of Jeff's life.

They met on a beach in France when Sarah had just finished college and was celebrating with some of her friends. In his early thirties and working for his Uncle Ben at the time, he had been on a trip with his Uncle to look over some materials that might be suitable to import for Ben's business. It was a dream trip to Jeff, and then he had met Sarah.

For the next two weeks they spent every minute together that Jeff could be away from Ben. He had fallen in love immediately because she was so lovely, outgoing, and fun to talk to. Certain that Sarah was the one, a proposal of marriage was blurted out the last night they were together, and she laughed and said she would think about it. They had grown so close, he was afraid to leave and risk her meeting someone else, so right before boarding the plane the proposal was repeated.

Thinking of nothing else for the next week until her flight landed in the United States, Jeff made future plans mentally on how their life would be together. Her parents met her at the airport, so she asked him not to be there. She would introduce him to them as soon as she thought it was suitable.

Jeff knew that Sarah's family had a great deal of money and didn't think that her parents would approve of an apprentice in his Uncle's business. He made a good living for his family's standards, but his paycheck would not impress her family, so he accepted a job with one of his Uncle's contractors. The job paid enough to support Sarah, and they would be able to save for the future. Jeff intended to go up rapidly in the new organization gaining a higher level status quickly and hopefully one day becoming a member of the 'club'.

The eight months the couple was together were thrilling. Believing they were absolutely soulmates, he did everything to make her happy. The focus was always on fun events such as amusement parks, concerts, and long walks around the lake downtown. The time passed quickly, and each day was an adventure for both.

He was on the verge of asking Sarah to marry him and live happily ever after when one night she started to act as if something heavy was on her mind. He asked what was wrong, and Sarah told Jeff she might be pregnant. Hoping in her heart he would be pleased, the only response heard was anger because he was thinking of the plans he had made for them. Without considering what was being said before speaking, the first statement blurted out was that he wasn't ready to have children. He was working too hard to get promoted at his job to have time for kids and considered the situation all Sarah's fault because she hadn't taken precautions. He told her coldly she should get rid of it.

That idea shocked Sarah so much she turned her back to him. Jeff didn't comprehend how much those words hurt as she was looking forward to having a family. From the first moment they met, he never understood that she didn't care at all about the money or what her family thought, but she wanted a family with the man of her dreams. Until that moment, she had thought Jeff was that man.

After she regained her composure, she turned and said that if they were going to have a baby, she would never do what he suggested. The fight lasted a half hour, and Jeff slammed the door as he walked out.

He wandered the streets thinking about the things they had said to each other. For hours he stayed angry believing she had planned the entire thing to trap him into starting a family immediately because she loved children. No, this fight certainly was not his fault, and she would have to change her attitude if she wanted to keep him. She had spoiled his proposal, and she should have thought about what she was doing.

Stopping by one of his former hangouts, two old friends were sitting at the bar. Sliding in next to them, a drink was ordered as well. He didn't mention Sarah but listened while his friends talked about their careers and how they were doing better each year. Then they both told him they had gotten married and had children. Jeff noticed that the two men seemed very happy and were doing very well.

"I guess I started out slower than they did," he thought. "If they were in my shoes, they would feel the same way I do. They are the same age as I am, but they had more opportunity once we got out of school, and their parents encouraged them to do well. I was lucky that my Uncle Ben asked me to work for him and become his apprentice. I would have no experience if it wasn't for him."

When the bartender told everyone it was last call, Jeff told his friends to keep in touch and began the walk home. Admitting to himself that it had been a long, rough week, he knew Sarah was being forced to take the brunt of the disappointments that accumulated during the last few days. The job wasn't going well, and the money wasn't coming in as fast as expected. Being told he might have a child on the way added enough pressure to make the stress too much setting the stage to take all of his frustrations out on her. He knew an apology would be given as soon as he walked through the door.

Unlocking the entrance to their home, the light switch was flicked on and the keys were thrown on the table. Everything was quiet, so he went into the bedroom to wake Sarah and tell her he was sorry. She wasn't there. He called her phone, but there was no answer, so he waited. He tried calling her each hour all night long, and at nine the next morning, she answered her phone.

"I am so sorry," he began.

Sarah interrupted him immediately, "I took a test from the pharmacy this morning, and I am not pregnant."

Jeff felt a rush of relief but didn't say a word about being happy. "I don't care as long as I know you are all right," he told her.

"I am fine," she said. "But Jeff, I have been thinking about it, and I just don't think this arrangement is going to work out. We really haven't taken the time to explore other relationships and grow as much as we should before making a solid commitment. We need to stretch ourselves a bit before making a final decision about the rest of our lives. I'm sorry, but I have decided to move on, so I will be picking up my things when you are at work. I don't want to see you anymore."

Jeff sat down quickly. She couldn't be serious. "Sarah, I said I was sorry. I didn't mean what I said, and I don't want you to leave. We don't have to get married right away, and we can explore many more things before taking our vows, but don't just leave like this. I was tired, and the job isn't going as well as I hoped it would. We will be fine, as you said this is just an adjustment period until we both fully discover ourselves."

Sarah was crying silent tears on the other end of the phone. She loved Jeff with all of her heart, but she didn't want a relationship where there was arguing and fighting, and she knew Jeff could be a hothead. The fact that he would even think of aborting a child had made her sick to her stomach. "Well, I think we should discover ourselves in different ways, but not together. I'm sorry Jeff, but our relationship just isn't going to work out. You will do fine on your job or on anything you decide to take on. I have been thinking about this for some time, and I am certain this is the right thing to do. We can be friends and stay in touch if you want to, but I am going to move back in with my parents and start dating other people. Take good care of yourself." Sarah hung up.

She had spent most of the night crying because she knew she was going to have a baby, and she knew that he didn't want it. Sarah wondered how life would be with a husband who didn't want to come home because he had a family that was holding him back. Her heart was broken, but she was not going to start a family under the conditions that he had set and the words he had spoken from his heart.

He stared at the phone for a minute once he realized they were disconnected, and then he became defensive and angry again. From that minute on, he swore he would not let anyone else put him through that again, and he would always keep the upper hand on his emotions.

He knew telling her to get rid of a child had been a very bad decision and wondered how he could have said that. He felt ashamed, but as always the selfishness and justification began and he told himself it was the only good choice at the time. Not once did he see that he was putting worldly matters in front of the people he loved. The inner voice he often heard said he might be wrong, but being certain he was right he left it at that without questioning the decision.

A year and a half later, he saw Sarah on the street with a man who was pushing a baby carriage. Jeff stood there with his mouth open, and as they approached, Sarah introduced her husband and their baby. Feeling very angry inside, he could barely speak. His heart said he still loved Sarah, but his mind said that she didn't deserve to be loved and he would never forgive her. She must have gotten a new boyfriend right away and went ahead with starting a family. Jeff quickly said hello and offered an excuse as to why he had to get going. In his anger, he never noticed that the baby had his hair and nose.

A few months later, one of his friends told him Sarah had married a friend of her Aunt's. He had been interested in Sarah for a long time, and he was quite a bit older than she was and also quite rich. The judgement made, of course, was that she must have wanted money all along, and he never let the anger go. By choosing to love, the lesson that loving someone can be painful had been learned. He had made up his mind at that point to never love anyone like that again. It was better to find people he liked being with and using them before they used him.

Coming back to the present time, every detail that had happened eight years before was so clear. Funny how things happened that could not be controlled; events that made you remember the past even if you didn't want to. Jeff stood up and walked to the window. Before him was a panoramic view of the entire city, and he could see people walking around Lake Eola. He liked that lake and had spent many nights walking around it thinking about his future.

Then his thoughts turned to Emily. He had met her last year, and he swore he would never wonder what was happening in Sarah's life ever again. This was the new beginning of his future, and he didn't want to waste a minute.

"Good morning, Jeff," Ms. Etonly said as she walked briskly into the room. "I am sorry that I kept you waiting, but our Board is meeting this afternoon and there was business that could not wait." She motioned for him to sit down while she walked to her desk and took a seat.

"That is fine," he told her allowing his memories to fade away. "I am thankful that you have a few minutes to speak to me about the funding for our educational research. I believe you will understand that the projects we are currently working on will enrich education tremendously and help all different types of children learn much more in a much shorter span of time." He smiled at her in his very charming way as she thumped her pencil on the desk.

"How much funding are you looking for, Jeff?" she asked with a peculiar smile on her face.

"I was hoping that Sun Dialee would contribute two million dollars this year to support our work," he answered. "We are talking with other organizations and foundations as well, and we have had three foundations offer funding for our use.  I want to ensure this work goes on and our children are taken care of for years to come."

"Did you bring along your business plan or the work breakdown structure and timeframes of the projects that have begun or will begin shortly?" she said waiting for a reply.

Jeff smiled at her and opened his briefcase.  He knew she would want this information to take to the Board, and he was more than eager to give this to her.  He felt that the money was his for certain.  "Here is a portfolio containing the information for two of our projects.  If you would like reports or data on more of our undertakings or if you would like me to do a presentation to the Board, I would be more than happy to accommodate any requests that you might have.  Perhaps a site visit would also be beneficial."

She pulled her glasses from the top of her head and slid them down to the end of her nose as she began to scan the documents handed to her.  Taking a few minutes to glance over the information and then looking back at Jeff she said, "I will take these to the Board meeting this afternoon.  As soon as I receive an answer from the members, I will let you know.  Thank you for coming."  She stood ending the meeting and shook the visitor's hand before he turned to walk out the door.

Jeff felt very positive as he left her office and gave the assistant a big smile.  Knowing Ms. Etonly could be tough, he also knew their business targeted young scholars to take under their wing and groom to become attentive business people for leadership roles in their organization.  He believed positive news would be heard from this corporation by the end of the week or possibly the first of the next week.

Whew, he was glad that was over, and it gave him confidence for the meeting coming in two hours with another organization that could certainly afford to offer a contribution.  His planning and collecting the right amount of information to present to each business was the precise path to take. Once all of the interviews were over, he would sit back and wait for the funding to come in. At that moment, all that could be felt was that there was no goal he couldn't achieve.

# CHAPTER FOUR

That day, Jeff was able to meet with three more executive officers who were considering funding for his research company. He understood that the economy was not doing very well at the time, and there were many other businesses requesting support to keep alive. With multiple education issues reported throughout the news weekly and educational techniques considered not effective, Jeff felt that he had a good chance to obtain at least a portion of the funding that was needed. He had every intention to continue asking, and to his surprise, the CEO of Genaby asked him to bring Emily to a pool party at his beach front house the very next Saturday.

The invitation was very impressive knowing that good contacts could be made at the function. He didn't expect the Board members at this organization to offer any funding, but the CEO had many friends who ran huge companies, and they might be good targets for support possibilities.

After Jeff left Genaby, he stopped by an advertising company whose director, Ralph, was a personal friend. Ralph stopped what he was doing when his buddy walked through the door and took the time to talk about the research, development and publishing company that his friend was running.

The two talked in length about ways to increase the money coming in and promoting the business until everyone knew its name and what the service and products could do for students. Ralph suggested looking into turning the company into a non-profit for tax purposes, and knowing about business loopholes, Ralph began to discuss the possibility of different options for streamlining payments that had to be made, depth of service projects that were to be accomplished, and how to make friends with the correct people to gain contracts. Jeff listened with interest and made a mental note to check out these avenues with his attorney and financial advisor. Of course more money in his pocket would be nice if the business could still grow. He thanked Ralph for the advice and told the advertiser he would be in touch.

Remembering when Ben had introduced them, Jeff thought back to his first impression of Ralph. He liked the marketing expert, but his Uncle told him firmly that Ralph would do anything to gain power and money. Ben had worked with Ralph for a few years but then dropped the advertiser because he didn't like the shoddy way Ralph did business or the liberties he took with others' money and information. Believing business people should be honest and use integrity in their dealings with others, Ben told Jeff to steer clear of the marketing guru.

Ralph had gotten into trouble a few years back after he skewed the accounting records of his agency and again when he billed a customer for a greater sum than the customer owed for the work that was accomplished. There were multiple complaints about him from the people who utilized his company's services, but Ralph escaped prosecution on all counts and continued on with his normal way of doing business.

Jeff believed Ralph was dishonest, but then again, he thought most business people were. His Uncle was the only one he knew who had high morals, but Ben was from a time past. In the current day, making money was accomplished through any means available even if integrity and morals had to be pushed aside. Yes, he would work with Ralph and use his friend's expertise to further his business, but he did have to make certain nothing went too far. He wanted to stay inside the boundaries where it wasn't too late to turn back and make the entire business completely honest. That way, he could manipulate while ensuring the business' survival. His mind was set and the decision was made to take this path and then correct the residual consequences later when the business was firmly planted and making lots of money.

Just then, his Uncle's face flashed through his mind. Jeff knew that the way he was thinking was wrong and that type of behavior was opposite of what he had always been taught. An interior voice told Jeff to consider the actual consequences, but the voice was brushed aside certain that he was just imagining things after the long day.

The justification process began again in his mind saying that in today's market he had no choice if success was the goal. The only thing he had to ensure was that he didn't go too far in working around the system. That satisfied his conscience, and he continued on the way home.

It was already after eight when he walked into the house tired and hungry. Emily wasn't there, and he started to get upset. Why wasn't dinner waiting for him? Picking up the phone, the pizzeria down the street was called and a large deluxe was ordered. Just as the call ended, Emily walked through the door looking as if she was a little upset herself. "What's the matter with you?" Jeff asked.

"I waited an hour for you at the church," Emily said, "then I just gave up. I didn't discuss any of the arrangements with Fr. Lore, and we didn't set a date. I want to make certain you can make it to the wedding before I do that."

They stood there looking at each other. Finally, Emily took off her coat and put the paperwork for her wedding plans in the den. She started for the kitchen to begin dinner, and before Jeff could commence talking about his hard day and no dinner waiting for him, the doorbell rang. Emily shook her head as she turned and walked to the door. It was the pizza man. She went to the side table to get her purse to pay him, and he thanked her as she closed the door. Without saying another word, she took the food into the kitchen and made a salad. Setting the table quickly, they both sat down with a glass of wine and ate silently.

After three pieces of pizza, Jeff threw down his napkin and went into the living room to watch the nightly news. He liked to keep up on what was going on daily, especially if any news concerned his donors. Emily slowly stood up feeling like her heart was too heavy to allow her to move, but she sluggishly began clearing the table.

She knew Jeff worked very hard, but she did expect him to put her first. This type of behavior had happened before, in fact, too many times before, and Emily was wondering if it was her. "Maybe he really doesn't love me," she thought. "Wouldn't he be interested in our wedding and be happy to plan it with me if he did? Maybe I am just pushing him too quickly and he really isn't ready for this yet. I don't want to continue living like this though. It just isn't right. Going to Reconciliation at church used to always help me, but until Jeff and I stop living as husband and wife when we are not, Confession will do me no good." She took the last of the dishes towards the kitchen, and turning the corner, she stopped to look back at Jeff one more time. She was perplexed.

Coming from a devout Catholic family, prayer time each evening had been on her family's schedule since she could remember, and she continued to pray even though she knew her living arrangements were not according to God's law. It made her sad at times to choose between God and Jeff, and hoping they could be married soon, her plan was to go to Reconciliation and start living according to God's edicts as soon as the vows were taken. Emily's parents were not happy at all with the arrangement, and her father always asked Jeff his intentions when they were together.

"What if I die living like this?" Emily asked herself. "I wouldn't go to Heaven, so I had better decide soon what I am going to do. Putting Jeff or anything else before God should never happen, and this is not what I want in my life." Inside, she already knew what she was going to do if Jeff did not come around soon. In fact, she had planned to talk about this very situation that night and how she felt, but now she knew any attempt for this discussion that evening was futile.

"God, please help me," she prayed. "I love You and want to be a good servant for You, and I love Jeff too. Please help me and don't let me be lost to hell. Thank you." Emily climbed the stairs to get ready for bed with a burden on her shoulders she could barely carry.

They had met early the year before at a party. One of her friends introduced them, and they clicked right away. Jeff was busy with his business, but he had time for her then, and they had done many things together enjoying each moment. After six months of dating, they moved in together. Jeff knew how Emily felt about it, and he promised that they would be married within the next six months. The timeframe he promised had come and gone, and no arrangements had been started. Soon Thanksgiving and the Christmas season would come so all arrangements would be pushed back again.

Her parents were adamant that she move back with them, and once they were married they could live together and make a home. Emily knew her parents were right, so bad mood or not, the next day she would bring up the subject and insist they solve the problem. If the issue was that he didn't love her, she wanted to know that now. If he did, perhaps they could elope and fix the problem quickly. She didn't want to blame Jeff any longer knowing what they were doing was wrong, and it was her decision to go along with it. Going downstairs to kiss him goodnight, she was tired to the bone and knew she must change her life.

The next morning Jeff was already up fixing breakfast when Emily came down the stairs. "We got invited to a pool party on Saturday," he told her. "We need to go because there will be business people there to meet who might help with the funding I am looking for. Are you going to work today?"

Emily was still in her robe, and she hadn't even started to get ready for work. She was a designer with a large company that made clothes for many of the big department stores. Loving the job and being very good at it, her dream had always been to study in Paris and maybe move there to run her own business one day. After she met Jeff, her dream faded, and her concentration turned to life with him.

"Yes, I am going in, but a little late," she said. "I want to talk to you before you leave."

"I don't have time for that this morning," he said. "If this is going to be a long discussion, maybe we can talk about it this weekend when we have more time. By the way, I am sorry about the church last night. I totally forgot about our appointment, but I will make it up to you. Do you have another appointment set up?"

She looked him squarely in the eye and said, "This discussion cannot wait until this weekend. I can't continue to live like this, and this is not what we agreed on when we moved in together. You know how I feel about these living arrangements without being married, so I am going to move back in with my parents. If you still want to get married, we can make another appointment with Fr. Lore and plan the wedding. I am packing up today and moving out." She never flinched when she spoke, but her words were kind and caring.

Jeff sat down and looked at the spoon in his hand. "You know I don't need this right now. Look, if you want to move out move out, but this business has to come first right now. What kind of life will we have if we don't make a great deal of money? I want vacations in Europe, a large home here, and a vacation home in the West. Our kids should go to private schools, and we will want to send them to the best universities. We have to think about the future. Besides, you know that what you learned in church as a kid has changed dramatically.

Society has evolved, and the meaning of what you studied in catechism has transformed over time to meet the needs of the current culture. We don't live in the desert or climb mountains to fast, and our world thinks and acts differently than what it did when that Bible was written. You have to grow with the times Em."

Emily looked at him as if she didn't even know him. "Funny, that is just what they are teaching at the universities and throughout lower level schools too. The current ideal is that each individual needs to do what they feel they need to do, and that is called being free or for most people liberalism. Yes, that is what everyone needs to do is their own thing and tell God how He should think. That does make the most sense doesn't it?"

Jeff looked over at her like she was losing her mind. She was being old fashioned and ridiculous. But Emily continued, "Do you realize you never once mentioned love in this conversation. Love is what makes any home happy, it is what makes people grow closer, and love will teach our children what they need to really learn. You forget Jeff that we are all on a journey through this life on earth. Our job is to become close to God and help others become close to Him while we are traveling down our path. Once our life on this earth ends, we go to the next life which will be what we choose from our life here. Our job isn't to make the rules and tell God how it is going to be. Yes, I am moving out today. You just gave me the answer to how you really feel, and I want you to be happy not just marry someone so you have a partner to take to your rich friends' parties. I know that you are Catholic like me, and I wish you would start going back to church for your sake, not mine. I plan on taking the time to go to Reconciliation today, and I hope you will take time out to do that as well. None of us knows how long we have on this earth." She went back up the stairs to pack.

Jeff couldn't believe that she was being so petty. He was almost killing himself trying to create a life they would both appreciate in the future. If she still enjoyed working in the years ahead, she could continue, or she could stay at home and be well taken care of. "Well, let her go. Maybe that is the right thing for now. She will come around to her senses once she starts missing me, and then we will make the arrangements and get married. Why is everything so hard!" He turned off the stove and ate the breakfast. After the plate was clean, the dishes were put in the sink, and a goodbye was loudly sent up the stairs as he left for the office.

For the next month he was busy from morning to night. The funding that he had been waiting for came through, and he was considering an expansion of his research right in Orlando. He tried to call Emily several times, but she never answered her phone, and then he forgot to call her for days at a time when he got busy with something else. He was surprised that there was never a message on his phone from her, but he knew she was busy with the new line of clothes that was to come out soon. It never dawned on him that she might be gone for good.

Spending more time at the office became the normal day, and he was working hard on a new research project with his chief designer, Brett. Finally, they were just about to finish the latest design when his phone rang, "Hello," he said trying to listen to both Brett on the last phase before testing and the caller on the other end of the line.

"Hi Jeff, its Ralph. I want to talk to you about a way to make more profit from what you produce. Got time to come see me tonight?"

"Sure," Jeff said. "How about eight?" They both agreed and hung up. Turning back to listen to the rest of what the designer had to say, he knew that the project they were working on was the best that had been developed yet.

Besides doing straight calculations and having a separate writing class, a plan had been made for the designers to develop courses and tests that combined math with writing that explained in detail why the calculations were important and how the results could be used. He felt that students would retain the information more fully if they utilized the lessons to learn the subjects in-depth, and Brett agreed. Once all of the issues had been worked through and Jeff knew the prototype would be completed that night, he decided to leave to meet his friend.

Walking to the door and waving goodbye, he wondered why Brett stayed so late so many nights. The designer had a family that rarely saw him lately, but the thought was that Brett felt like the business was his, and in a way it was because he would put his name on the design as well. He was thankful that he had found this designer and had chosen him from many that had applied for the position. Jeff smiled as he got into the car.

The night was foggy when he pulled up outside of Ralph's house. The moon was strangely colored with wisps of black streaking it on a downward angle. He watched the movement of the clouds for a few minutes and noticed that there were clouds moving in all different directions which was quite rare. Jeff felt uneasy and thought about just going home when the garage light came on and Ralph stood in the large doorway.

"Glad you made it," he said to his visitor, "come on in." He led Jeff through the house to the dining room, "I have been doing some calculations, and I think we can make some good money with the strategy I have come up with." They sat down at the table where Ralph had papers strewn across the top.

"Look at this," he told Jeff. "I know that you are going to expand to all corners of the world sooner or later, so I took the figures that you compiled showing how much it cost to research, develop, and

29

publish the elementary grammar books. I looked over each book to see what would need to change for the states and overseas cultures. I know it is important to get pictures and concepts right so the particular target audience receives what they need. Being in a business where the owner sends me on trips worldwide, I have met people who contract out for this type of material to send to places like India, China, and so forth. We use the cost to produce and publish and then add handling, packaging, logistics, and administrative costs. We cut the training manuals, workbooks, and tests down so there is a minimum amount of material. Those receiving the information will be able to use it they just won't know the difference in what they got to what is developed. This plan begins after we sell the materials and the regulations are satisfied, then we start to cut down what is included currently and ship the inferior product. This plan can include customers all over the world, and I know we can get away with this because the buyers all work with bottom line numbers and purchase what there is money for. Of course, the product is bundled with many copies inside, but not one that I have ever worked with breaks down by item what they are getting for the contract. The product is received and then sold and shipped just as it was when it came in."

Both men stood looking at the figures that had been calculated, and then the advertiser continued, "The materials will not be created for detailed educational purposes. That means you will have to make more filler contents such as pictures, and when we cut the material down, move the excess to another book that we can sell separately. We can make a killing on this." Ralph started to rub his hands together like an old miser waiting to count his coins.

Jeff looked at him as if he were crazy. "No, no," Ralph said, "pay attention this can work and can add millions to the profit margin. I know what I am talking about."

Jeff sat back in the chair and didn't know what to say. He looked at Ralph and then back at the table feeling quite uncomfortable. This was definitely fraud, and he wondered how many years in prison he could get for doing this. He planned to skim a little money for himself, but he didn't plan to be that unethical and present one manual for the sale and then cut the materials back to give less to the students.

He understood exactly what his friend was suggesting and also knew Ralph's idea would generate as much money as he had calculated. The business would never be able to realize this much profit in many years at its current rate of return, so Jeff began to consider mentally what the path forward should be. Psychological reasoning began.

The costs would increase to send the materials overseas. The buyers would purchase materials that would still offer solid teaching tools, even though less than advertised, and sell to customers who had the funds to buy them. Of course, some of the overseas countries and some areas of the United States would not need the same caliber materials that were used in higher income areas. Being poor, they would have few skills to enhance, and the materials, no matter how complete, may not even be able to increase the students' chances to make a difference in their lives. He decided that the children would not be cheated.

After mulling over his thoughts for a few minutes, Jeff looked at Ralph and slapped his friend on the back, "I think this is a great idea. We can handle the regulations here, and as you said, most other countries probably don't have standards. When do we get started?"

Both men started to laugh. This was business and creative thinking was necessary to progress in this dog eat dog world. Ralph, of course, would be a consultant and would receive a fee for his part in this scheme, but Jeff knew that he would benefit tremendously as well.

If everything went as planned, they could continue to expand this strategy until they reached all parts of the world.

Jeff left Ralph's house that night whistling a tune. He hadn't done that in ages and forgot all about the odd sky that had appeared that evening. Pulling into the driveway, he got out of the car with a burst of energy and leaped up the steps, opened the door, and turned on the lights. His phone had been silenced, so taking it out to turn the ringer back on he saw that someone had called. The number was Emily's.

It had been months since she left, and they had spoken only a few times. He told her before that he still wanted to get married and that they should set up the arrangements. She wanted to wait for him to become more serious and put some effort into the wedding plans. Maybe she thought they had waited long enough.

For some reason the motivation just wasn't there to talk with her about the wedding as it had been before. He loved her but had so many other things to work on that taking the time out to plan a wedding wasn't interesting now. Maybe waiting longer would put more excitement into the relationship and planning. Well, he wasn't going to call her back tonight.

Instead, he decided to call Brett. Dialing the designer's home phone, he walked to the kitchen to get a drink while it rang. Finally, one of the kids answered and Jeff asked for Brett. He heard the child yell for her dad and Brett said hello. Jeff began, "We made a lot of progress today. Things are picking up and are going the right way. I was talking to my advertising guy, and he came up with some suggestions that can help the business' bottom line." The boss continued and explained how all of the manuals they developed would be produced, and once approved the material would be cut down for each target audience. They needed to do that immediately after approval, and then the extra material would be taken and another manual with the sections they had removed would be put together to sell.

Brett said, "Jeff, are you certain you want to do that? That is dishonest and unlawful."

Jeff didn't say anything for a minute and then told the designer it was the best route to take. The important part was that the customers would get all of the information that had been approved, just in a different format. Brett didn't buy it and told Jeff he really didn't want any part of the scheme.

"Look Brett," he tried to sound convincing but firm, "we need to make more money so we can expand this business and make it solid. It will ensure all of the jobs at the labs and publishing house that we have now and should increase the number of people in the future."

Brett understood that he was being directed without discussion. "Is that a type of threat concerning my continuing employment?" Brett asked.

"Look, I need people who follow directions so I can run the business the way I need to," Jeff answered and then told Brett he would see him the next day. If he still had issues with the decision they could discuss it.

Brett knew Jeff well enough to know that he would have to do as directed and break the law or look for another job. Hanging up the phone and considering options, his mind went to the mouths he needed to feed. That didn't relieve his conscience though.

Jeff felt as if all would be well with Brett as the phone was turned off. The designer would just have to get used to the idea, and when the outcome from the changes was complete, he wouldn't think it was so bad. After tomorrow, they would be on the right track.

Running up the stairs, the shower was the first stop, and the hot water felt good. After drying off, he stretched out on the bed and turned on the TV to watch the news. The Middle East was in a new turmoil, and Palestine and Israel were firing on each other again. On the home front, some well deserving veterans were being honored for their service years ago. Jeff started to relax and began to drift off to sleep.

He smiled in his sleep as he saw himself dressed in a beautiful new suit. It was very expensive, and as the money continued to come in quickly, he had begun living extravagantly. A new multi-million dollar mansion was in the process of being purchased and a couple of very expensive cars as well. The strategy Ralph had come up with worked, and there was plenty of money for both of them.

He decided to stop at a party that one of his backers was having, and it was certain to be a high status affair. Walking in, he was greeted by the host who pointed down the hallway to two different doors. On the right, the positive atmosphere could be felt from those within, and the happiness generated from inside was tremendous making the feeling spread. The people were dressed in dazzling array and were all very cheerful and inviting. "Please come in," they said. "We have been waiting for you and are so glad that you are here." Jeff smiled and took a step toward the door wondering who these people were.

In the very next instant, a man dressed in black caught his arm and pulled him to the left. "Come this way, and you will find everything that pleases you." The man smiled at Jeff and ushered him toward the door on the left.

A person from the right stood in the doorway and said to him, "Do not enter there, for through that doorway is only earthly pleasure and heartache. Come, set with us and we will discuss eternity."

Jeff was quite confused, and he looked through both doorways. On the right, the people were congregating, and they laughed and talked to each other as if they were all old friends. There was a feeling of contentment and peace where everyone relaxed and there was nothing to worry anyone.

Through the left door, he saw all different types of people wandering around. Some were in what looked to be deep discussions, and others stood by watching what was going on around them. They all had drinks in their hands and were enjoying a variety of different foods laid out on long tables. He could tell most of the people in the room had a great deal of money, and he heard one couple tell another about a long, luxurious trip they had taken before going to their summer home in the mountains.

The man in black pulled Jeff toward the left again and said, "You will find everything in here that you have always desired throughout your life."

Jeff began to follow the man, and the person across the hall made a plea to Jeff one last time, "Do not enter through that door and disregard this path. If you do, you may be lost forever."

He was perplexed but decided that the party on the left offered much more entertainment, and looking through the doorway again, he saw many women who were dressed beautifully and looked to be alone. He thought it over for a brief second and walked through the door on the left.

At the moment he entered the room, a tall man approached him and said, "We got the materials you sent that are to be shipped to China. Pretty shabby product and glad to see you cut down the size of what you originally promised. It will cost us less for shipping." He walked away laughing.

Jeff scanned the area and was amazed that the people looked quite different once he was in the room than they had when he was looking from the outside in. They became disgusting to look at, and the entire room turned dark and damp. The food smelled rotten, and there was a stench that he found very hard to tolerate. He decided this party was not what he thought it was, and he began to walk towards the door. Before he could cross the threshold to the hall leading to the other room, two large men came and stood between him and the doorway and said, "Ananias, you will not depart from here. You have thought only of yourself, and you have lied to God's children and offended the Holy Spirit."

Immediately as the men finished speaking, Jeff fell over dead. The men took him and threw him out of the wide door. He landed in the middle of a roadway that was deserted and very dark.

Suddenly back to life, he saw a man next to him who was nudging him. The man was tall and lanky, his smile was quite crooked, and there were only a few hairs on the top of his head. The suit he wore was expensive and of the latest style. His shoes shone so bright that a reflection could be seen.

"Hello," he said to Jeff. "I am Mr. Kleptes, and I have been sent to work with you. You have taken on quite a task of pilfering organizations out of their money to put into your pocket while not giving the products and services you promised. It was thought that I might be able to assist to expand your strategy."

Jeff turned to the man. "Who are you, and who has sent you to tell me that?"

"The great Diabolos sent me, and he likes the work that you have been doing. He believes that I can help you to achieve much more in a much wider area," Kleptes retorted smiling. "Please do not act as if you don't know what I am speaking of. We watch you carefully. Diabolos wants to groom you to become a great assistant, and as humans are very susceptible to greed, we are certain that you can produce many followers for him." Kleptes smiled again, and then he started to laugh.

Suddenly there were demons all around Jeff that were terrifying. They changed shapes as they moved around him, and they came closer and then moved away. Kleptes changed into one of them and stuck a pointed finger into Jeff's chest. "You will be just like us Ananias, and we are waiting for you to fall dead!" Kleptes threw his head back and laughed with the most evil outburst Jeff had ever heard.

Gasping for air as he was jolted out of sleep, he jumped out of bed with tears streaming down his face. Breath was coming sporadically and his body shook so hard calling 911 was considered. He swung around to see if they were still there, and there was no one in the room except him.

Sitting down on the edge of the bed he tried to calm down and catch his breath. Another horrible nightmare like the one before, and it frightened him so badly he didn't know where to turn. Denial began and his mind simply said that it was foolish to think the discussion with Ralph had anything to do with this, so he went over the rest of his day and decided it was an offshoot from the discussion with Brett. The designer was wrong and he knew that, so why had such a ghastly nightmare resulted from the talk?

Switching on all of the lights as if that would keep the hideous things away, he paced back and forth across the room. Slowly, the shaking lessened, and gradually total control of the trembling was accomplished. Maybe he should go see a psychiatrist. Maybe he was going out of his mind.

Calming down mentally, his thoughts went over the dream again. He recognized things that Ralph had planned out and he had agreed to, but the circumstances were different. Maybe the whole thing was because of the eerie night he noticed at Ralph's and the discussion they had. There were no movies or television shows that contained plots like the nightmare. He hadn't recognized anyone or anything except the teaching materials that had been brought up, and earthly pleasure was all that anyone in the world could hope for. Why the things in the left room turned rotten or different after he entered was a mystery. Life on earth was just starting to take shape for him and living was going to be sensational.

He discarded the memories of the right side and what the person had said about eternity. Talking about another existence so far away from today was just not something Jeff wanted to do. He would think about his eternity when the time was right.

After believing he completely understood the actions in the dream, the conversations from the people he saw and the creature were attributed to business activities brought out of the subconscious, and the occurrences became inaccurate generating bad dreams that distorted real life. But he still felt uneasy inside, so he turned on the television and started to watch an old story about the Civil War. The pacing continued, and the movie neglected to take his mind somewhere else even though the meaning of the nightmare had been explained.

# CHAPTER FIVE

By morning, Jeff had settled down completely and knew that he had been working too hard for the past few months. Add to that the junk food eaten while on the run and of course that would set him up for nightmares. The only thing he could not figure out was why the dreams always included the same type of creatures. He shrugged off the thought and decided to return Emily's call. It would be good to hear her friendly voice.

"Hi Jeff," she answered right away. "I was wondering if we could meet for lunch." He told her lunch would be fine, and that they could meet at Radcliff's at noon. Feeling a little lost as to what he would say when they met, he hung up and turned to the draft of the math book that had been published the day before.

As the material was scanned, he began to see more clearly what Ralph had meant about cutting out portions and publishing a second book that would contain the removed parts. The material that would be taken out was critical, and the schools would have to buy the next book to make up for the missing instruction. Genius is what he considered Ralph's idea to be.

Beginning to mark several paragraphs to cut from the current version, his phone rang, and looking over to see if the caller was important enough to answer, the screen said it was Ms. Etonly. "Good morning," he said with a smile answering immediately.

"Good morning Jeff," she responded. "Our Board wants you to show some of the material from your research to a number of principals from the local schools so that they can discuss if the outputs will justify the money that will be spent to develop the new educational manuals. We would like to meet with you Thursday, two days from now, if that is possible. My secretary will contact you for the location and time of the meeting."

"Of course we can do that," he said very vibrantly and confidently. "Just let me know the specifics and we will be there."

"Fine; thank you," and she hung up.

Jeff looked at his watch. It was ten in the morning and Tuesday. That didn't give them much time to get the materials printed and a presentation of their business plan created. The breakdown structure of outreach to the targeted markets was needed as well.

"Hi Brett," Jeff said calling his chief designer. A detailed list of everything that had to be accomplished and reviewed by Thursday morning was rattled off so they could be ready for the meeting. Brett knew how important this was to the organization as well as his own survival, so he told Jeff he would get Sam to start publishing the full version books that Jeff had approved and would then begin on the presentation. He assured his boss that everything would be ready on time and would be very convincing and appropriate for the audience they would be addressing.

Jeff started out the door to get to the lab. Every pair of hands would be needed to ensure everything that had to be done would be, and then he remembered Emily.

"Hi Em," he said getting into his car. "Listen, I can't make lunch today. I just got a call from Etonly and she wants me to meet with multiple principals from local schools on Thursday. It will take all day and night for the next two days to pull this off. Sorry, but I am going to have to cancel lunch. Can we talk next week?"

Emily sighed and told him that would be fine. Putting the phone down, she knew for certain that they were through for good. She didn't want to admit that but could no longer fool herself into thinking she would ever be first in his life. Tears flooded her eyes but were quickly wiped away. She had a life too and wasn't going to give up important principles to accommodate anyone. Deciding to move on, dates would be accepted from this point forward when others asked her to go out with them.

Jeff forgot about Emily as soon as he put the phone in his pocket. Although he had received some support from Etonly's Board, it had not been as much as he had hoped for. The call meant that they were considering quite a bit more funding if he could satisfy everyone's concerns at the meeting. This was just the break he had been waiting for.

Brett had already come up with a list of topics that would be discussed and some examples that would be included. Jeff went through and rearranged where he felt it was necessary and then added a few areas that he thought would be critical to address. Once the topic list was complete, they began the slides that Jeff would present and speak to in detail during the talk to the chosen audience.

After several hours of creating slides and adjusting as they went along, Brett pushed his chair back. Jeff looked at him and asked him if he was alright. Brett nodded and said he just needed a few minutes and got up and went to the break room to get a cup of coffee.

Jeff paced back and forth thinking about what they had written and decided they would stop while he went through the briefing to see if the presentation was smooth and confident. Brett could ask questions, and changes could be made where necessary. That would tell him if they were going in the right direction or if something else needed to be developed more in-tune to the target audience.

Sitting back in the chair, Brett told his boss he was ready, and Jeff began to present the slides. The first two or three felt like they addressed exactly what they should. After that, the presentation just wasn't detailing what the principals needed to know. They both agreed that changes would have to focus on each subject and what the materials would do for the students.

Jeff knew they would have to be careful here. He couldn't present the manuals as being the absolute final draft of what the students would get. He would have to talk around the fact that adjustments were pending and the result may lead to a second manual, but no mention of purchasing another book for the students to get the full impact would be given while discussing what the materials would offer.

He brought this up to Brett, and the designer looked at him as if he was insane. "You can't do that, that is fraud," he began. "The students need all of the material that was developed together in order for them to learn correctly. If you tear the books into two parts, the kids will lose too much in the transition and will not benefit nearly as well as they would from the way that we created the learning tools. You just can't do that and show the full version to the people Thursday leading them to believe the students will be given the enlarged version when they will not unless two books are purchased." He stared at his boss as if he had lost his mind.

"I understand what you are saying Brett, but the separation of materials will boost much needed sales. We not only need to develop educational materials and publish them, we also have to come up with smart business practices to ensure the company survives and continues to provide for students."

The two looked at each other for a long minute. Jeff sensed that Brett was considering whether to walk out or stay. Neither one wanted to compromise but they both needed each other and the owner knew the designer was one of the best in the field. His pride would not let Brett tell him how to run his business even though logic said that the material creator knew what students needed much more clearly than what he did.

Jeff had not contemplated this event in his planning. He had to keep Brett to ensure any technical questions from the people who would be at the briefing could be answered effectively. Brett had developed the material, so another person would not be as passionate or know how to explain fully what had been considered during the development.

"Look," Jeff said, "we can discuss the pros and cons of this later. I don't want to lose you, so I am willing to negotiate the final product. For now, we need to sell these publications so we can pay everyone's salary. Let's get this done and go to the meeting and see what happens. If we don't do well, the word will spread and we won't have to worry about it. It will give us both time to think things over."

Brett agreed and turned back to the computer. The next slide appeared and the two discussed each point on the slide and then changed what was not appropriate. They continued through the rest of the slide deck and started to discuss the materials they would distribute to make their points.

That night and the next day were spent working hard to ensure every topic was covered. Sometime during Wednesday, Etonly's secretary called to say the meeting would be the next day at two-thirty and would take place in the conference room at Etonly's insurance office.

Wednesday night about midnight, Jeff told Brett to go home and get some rest for the next day. They would meet at the insurance office at two o'clock, and hopefully everything would go well. Brett waved goodbye as he walked out the office door, and Jeff sat dazed wondering if they had done a good enough job to get the extra funding that was being considered. If they did really well, the principals would talk to other organizations about funding assistance too. If they did poorly, well, he would have to rethink the business.

Suddenly he experienced searing heartburn. Breaking out into a cold sweat, he sat still for a few minutes wondering what he had eaten or drank to make him suffer this way. Then his thoughts turned to having an internal problem. Being sick at this time with an ulcer or something else wouldn't work. Slowly, the bad sensations began to subside, and he started to feel normal. After about twenty minutes, all of the pain had gone, and he got up grabbing the presentation to take home and review one more time. This was no time to feel bad, so the unwanted burning was pushed to the back of his mind. The people who would be at the briefing and the concepts that would sell the materials to those watching went through his tired mind.

Once at home, the shower was turned on, and the hot water felt so good his body started to relax. The muscles in his neck began to loosen, and letting the water continue to beat against his stressed body seemed to be working well. Once the water was turned off, he walked over to the bed and fell full length across it. He would just lay there for a few minutes and then get up and once again review the entire meeting that was set for the next day.

The phone rang, and his secretary asked him when he would be in and what time the published materials needed to be completed and packaged. He shook his head trying to think and told her he would call her the next day and let her know. She reminded him that the meeting was that very day.

Shooting out of bed not believing it was Thursday already, he looked at his phone and wondered what had happened to the hours since stepping out of the shower. Changing what was said before, she was told he would be at the office in an hour. The materials would have to be ready to go by one that afternoon.

There wasn't enough time to analyze what had happened. He hurried to the bathroom to shave, and gazing into the mirror, a tired looking face was reflected back. Oh no, this would have to be shaken off quickly.

Once the grooming was finished, he headed down to the kitchen in his robe to get some breakfast. Looking at the clock, the hour hand said it was ten, so breakfast needed to be eaten quickly, the new suit in the closet would be put on, and he would get to the office to ensure the briefing was printed and correct. The materials would also have to be checked to make sure everything was set to go. Dialing Brett's number to make certain he would be there on time, the designer confirmed he would meet his boss at the customer's location.

Jeff knew he needed to relax, so he began to think of his mother and how she would rock back and forth when she did the sewing. The rocking memory slowly calmed him down, and he ran up the stairs to get dressed and gather his confidence so he would do well that afternoon.

Both he and Brett arrived at the same time in front of the insurance headquarters, and each grabbed a bundle of materials and walked inside to the elevator. Giving the other one a smile, they stepped onto the lift and began the ride upstairs.

The secretary was ready for them and showed them into the conference room where they could prepare. The computer was on and the screen was down and ready to go. Jeff laid a manual at each seat that had a water glass, and in silence he started back through the slides.

Ms. Etonly walked into the room and asked both of the men if there was anything else they required. Both assured her everything was ready to go and they were fully prepared. She looked each one directly in the eye for a full minute to ensure herself everything would go smoothly and then walked out of the room.

In just a few minutes, people started to arrive and enter through the big, double conference room door. Jeff met each one as they came in, introduced himself and Brett, and discussed any issue that any of the attendees asked him. He stood tall and smiled looking like a confident leader. Most of the visitors were principals and quite impressed with the speaker for the day. They smiled and spoke positively of their expectations to the others around them. Ms. Etonly and Mr. Arthur, a Board member, did not act enthused, and they sat as if expecting a disaster to occur with the presentation.

Jeff began the briefing and Brett passed out further information on their business plan, organization structure, and funds that would be needed for each stage of business development. The slide deck told a good story, and the audience seemed to be following well and understanding all of the concepts.

Mr. Arthur raised his hand and asked about educational materials for disabled children. Jeff stopped the subject he had been addressing, and smiling, turned towards Mr. Arthur. "We have not taken on development of that type of educational material yet. Although we are planning to produce training for the disabled in the future, we have no timeframe set for that now, and no research has been accomplished in that area." Jeff waited for another response, but none came.

Mr. Arthur was not finished though and asked if the manuals they had been given as samples were exactly the manuals that would be sent to the schools.

Jeff looked at the manuals and then at Brett. "Yes, these manuals are very close to the manuals that will be shipped," he said smiling confidently.

Mr. Arthur did not like the body language he saw in the speaker before answering, so he pressed on. "All countries that are targeted will get this same material in their language?"

"Yes," Jeff answered again. Smiling at the audience, the presentation was continued. Finishing sooner than planned, he looked around the room and asked if there were any questions. No one responded.

Ms. Etonly stood up and started to clap lightly; the audience followed. "Thank you Jeff for the enlightening presentation. The

Board members will discuss all they have seen and make a final decision."

"One more thing," Mr. Arthur said. "Would you please meet the Board members at Lincoln school tomorrow at one to tour the classrooms of some of the children who would utilize your training? You can also get a clear picture if the material you are offering is correct for the audience."

Jeff accepted and told the man that he and Brett would certainly be there at that time to tour the school. After thanking everyone for their time, the two business men left the conference room.

They walked out to the parking lot and stopped by Brett's car. "I can't go to see the kids and answer questions like Arthur asked today and then go back to the lab and cut the manuals down," the designer said looking at his boss. "That is deceptive, and he will be watching. I won't take the chance of getting caught doing something that stupid when I have a family."

Jeff looked down at the ground and then into the eyes of Brett. "I know how you feel, and I don't want to commit fraud and go to prison either. We can work this out. Maybe we can leave the manuals as they are for this area and cut them down for other places in this country and overseas. Arthur would never know anything was wrong if we did that. We just have to be smart about it."

The designer looked over his shoulder as he moved to the driver's side of the car. "I'm going home, and I will see you at the school tomorrow. I mean it Jeff, this is too complicated, and I don't want to break the law and ruin my reputation." He got into his car and drove away.

The next day Ms. Etonly, Mr. Arthur, several other Board members, Jeff and Brett met at Lincoln school and walked into the principal's office together. "Good morning," the administrator smiled

49

at the group. "I have several classes that are expecting us to visit, so please let's get started."

They followed the man down a hall and turned to the right. He stopped in front of a classroom on the left and opened the door motioning everyone inside. "Good morning class. We have visitors today who are going to briefly learn about what is taught in your classroom. I know that you will explain to these fine folks exactly what is taught and what you would like to learn."

All of the guests stood in the back of the room, and the teacher began by showing the books utilized and the homework that the students completed from the books. The children appeared to be normal eight year olds, and a few of the students stood and addressed the group. They told what they liked most about their instruction and what they believed could be improved. Each student who spoke also told the visitors what they would like added to the training.

It was a pleasant experience for all, and the group thanked the children and waved as they left. The principal went back to the main hall with the guests following and turned to the left. Not far down the corridor, they stopped in front of a classroom that had a much larger door. Opening the entranceway, he ushered his guests inside, and they were all surprised at the children in the room.

Each child had some type of special need. There were only ten children allowed in each of these special rooms, and there was one teacher and two assistants who helped the kids with the school work developed especially for them. All of the visitors walked around the room, and each picked out a child to talk to and see what they were working on. It seemed like a happy classroom, and the adolescents appeared to enjoy their helpers.

The instructor explained a few of the learning tools that were utilized and demonstrated how the teacher, assistants, and children interacted. When she was finished showing them the current instruction, she went into the needs and shortcomings of what they had to work with and how different tools could be improved. Enhancements would make a world of difference she assured all.

Thanking everyone, the group exited the classroom and stood in the hall asking the administrator several questions that would help the attendees understand more thoroughly. The head of the school discussed the future plans they had for every child's need and how they were trying to gain grants and accommodate the requirements. As they reached the front door of the school, he invited the group back to observe more classrooms and possibly spend a day to watch the instruction given. They all thanked him for his time and waved as they walked towards the parking lot.

"Do you think you could come up with teaching tools for all different types of students?" Mr. Arthur looked at the two business men.

Jeff responded, "Of course, with enough time we certainly can accommodate. But that would take a great deal more funding and many more employees to research, develop, and publish instruction for every type of child. The manuals that we are currently producing are for average children of all different ages and in multiple languages because that is where the largest need is. Special needs children could be accommodated, but that would be years down the road."

Mr. Arthur nodded his head. He understood because he had been working with disabled children for multiple years. Many times he had approached businesses on the subject of training materials, but there was such a wide variety of needs that it was very hard for a company to concentrate on this type of research, development, and publishing and make a decent living off of it. When they did pursue this type of publishing, the materials became too expensive for the schools and other educational facilities to afford them. It was a very difficult situation, and one that Arthur intended to continue working on.

"Perhaps the key is to give more of the funding to the special needs education centers or begin a non-profit to design and publish what is needed," Arthur spoke his thoughts out loud, and everyone stopped to listen. "We will see about that. Thank you all for coming and seeing what I am especially concerned about. Perhaps designers like you can come up with new ways of accommodation," he said shaking Brett's hand.

Ms. Etonly told Jeff she would call him when the Board had made a final decision. She really couldn't tell him anything at that moment about what each of the Board members was considering, but she would keep in touch. Jeff thanked her, and the two business men continued to walk to the parking lot.

"I'll meet you at the office," he told Brett. "We can discuss any concerns you might have and then continue on with what we decide. Maybe we should have more staff in the room as well to get their thoughts."

Brett agreed and started his car. He was not happy about his job at the moment and wondered if he ever would be again. He loved what he did and wanted to make a good impact in the world of education, but he didn't want to sidestep what was important to ensure money was the emphasis.

The designer had grown up in a middle class home, and he and his family were comfortable but not rich. He didn't want to be rich with money but did want to know that he made a positive difference to others throughout his life. Being a good role model and teaching his children that as well was important. Unfortunately, his type of work was not in demand in this part of the country, and his family liked it here, so walking away from this job right now was not an option. This whole ordeal was quite upsetting to him.

Brett had talked to his wife about the situation and Jeff's plans previously. He explained to her that although what was going on was not right, he would have to go along until another job could be found. Feeling very upset, he had tried to calm down and assure her everything would be alright, but she insisted she could find a job to help out until he secured other work. That only upset Brett more because he wanted her home with the kids. He had been brought up with his mother at home, and that is the way he wanted his children to grow up. They agreed to pray about their problem, and they knew a path would be made for them.

Slowly turning into the research parking lot, the car was pulled into the parking space and a silent prayer that everything would work out was said. The door slammed as he entered the building, and Brett told his assistant Sam to get everyone together for a meeting with the boss.

Brett walked to Jeff's office and knocked on the door as he opened it. "I told everyone to gather in the conference room. Are you just about ready to go over what the future plans are and how we are going to handle them?"

Jeff nodded and started to gather some papers from his desk. He had already asked his secretary to set up the computer in the room so he could show everyone the presentation that they were going to discuss. Feeling very self-assured, he strolled to the meeting and said hello to everyone as he closed the door.

"Thank you all for stopping what you were doing on little notice to meet with me. I have been analyzing the goals that this company has and the different avenues that we can take to achieve these goals. Some targets are achievable more quickly than others, and some are more in line with what we want to eventually accomplish. In order to obtain the market share we need and be able to expand the business quite quickly, I have decided on several main goals. From these, we will build until we are in the right position to stretch ourselves and then plan strategies to accomplish the other goals which will then take us into the realm of a major player in the educational market."

Jeff pushed the button and the next slide appeared. "In order to realize our vision, every bit of the material development that all of you worked on and designed will be utilized to ensure all students will benefit the utmost from the pages. A change in plans comes when we take material out of the one manual for each subject area and make two manuals out of each subject area." He heard several people in the room gasp, so he hurried on. "Of course we will ensure that every student receives the training that was developed for them, so the only difference will be that they will be working from two different manuals, one and then another, instead of the originally planned one manual. Brett, who is the chief expert, will oversee splitting each manual into two. Some instruction books may already have a clean break in the middle where others may have to be rearranged to ensure the flow makes complete sense. I know that Brett is up to this task." Jeff continued through the slides and then turned to ask if there were any questions.

One hand went up, and the speaker pointed to the person to ask their question. "What happens if the school or facility does not provide the second manual? The children will benefit very little from half of the material only."

Jeff assured the team member that when selling the manuals the people ordering would absolutely know that both manuals must be ordered for the student to be able to realize the complete educational benefit.

Various other questions were asked, and he saw some people shaking their heads. Knowing that these people were very conscious of what they did, he knew they were concerned about excellent teaching devices versus mediocre tools and also knew that profit was not a huge consideration when good education was in question. To make certain none of his people walked out the door, he stopped taking questions that might further upset them and spoke to everyone.

"I know this is a little disappointing to you, but we did not receive all of the funding that was requested. Because of this, we must take some type of action to ensure our survival and that the company does not have to downsize. Every one of you continues to create the types of educational material that is needed by the public, so we will produce in a way that will keep our business going and satisfy learning requirements. As time goes by and more funding is secured, we can always go back to our original plan of one manual."

That seemed to satisfy just about everyone in the room. No one was concentrating on why two smaller manuals would earn a much greater profit and be cheaper to publish, but the thought that downsizing may have to occur took their focus off of students and put emphasis on their jobs. They clapped as Jeff finished and all trickled out of the room feeling as if they had won somehow while they discussed the ways they could accomplish what was being asked of them.

Jeff saw Brett's face after he had finished, and his designer appeared to be quite upset. He went to Brett's side and smiled, "Are you alright Brett? I know that you are concerned about this situation, but I went over the figures multiple times earlier, and this is the only way we can keep afloat. As I said, when funding increases, we will go back to selling one manual per subject."

The designer looked him straight in the eye and then walked out of the room. He hadn't said one word about quitting, so the CEO felt safe. Jeff had accomplished what he set out to do and didn't think the people would take any adverse action. The way he had presented the service agreements made all the difference in the world, and he smiled as he walked back to his office. He had won the first battle.

Brett began to feel unsettled once he reached his office, so he closed the door. He didn't want any part of what was going to happen, but he didn't know what to do about it. He couldn't change the owner's mind. Jeff was only driven by profits, but he was driven to follow what he believed in and that was to follow church teachings not man's beliefs. He wanted to practice God's laws, integrity, good morals, and humility. Nothing about this situation would bring respect from his family's eyes when they looked at him.

Sitting down in his chair, his head began to pound and his breathing became sporadic. He told himself to just calm down and think this through logically. There was a good solution to this whole thing, and thinking analytically about it was much better than looking at it emotionally.

After a few minutes, he started to feel better and decided to go home for the day. No meaningful work would be accomplished in the small amount of afternoon left, and he wanted to see his family. He stuck his head through Jeff's office doorway and told him he was leaving. "Will I see you tomorrow?" Jeff asked. Brett nodded and closed the door.

The owner leaned back in his chair and looked out of the window. Everything was starting to fall into place, and from this point forward, nothing should interfere with their plans. He would take care of everyone else after taking care of himself. Feeling assured that everything being done was absolutely acceptable he knew in the long run their plan would make things better for all. Once enough money was available, he could make the manuals even better and more comprehensive without raising the costs very much. Certain that this path was the right one, he knew customers and employees would profit from all this work and planning he was doing. Yes, one day he would be a hero to all.

# CHAPTER SIX

Two days after the meeting with Arthur and Etonly, Jeff was thinking about Emily and wanted to meet with her to decide where they were going from here. Things had been going well in life lately, and he wanted to fix this part too. He dialed her number and listened to it ring. She didn't answer, and he wondered where she could possibly be already this morning. The thought left his mind quickly, and he decided to leave her an apologetic message, "Good morning Em. I am sorry that I had to postpone our lunch and was wondering if we could meet tonight. I know that I have been neglecting you lately and am sorry. Please give me a call so we can have dinner together."

Emily watched her phone as the message registered and the screen went dark. There was no interest in her heart to listen to what he said. Her feelings for Jeff as a future husband had disappeared, and she wanted to move on with her life. What still concerned her was his soul. She didn't want him to continue living the way he had been but wanted him to change his life and put focus on what was important instead of money. Unfortunately, he would ignore anything she said on this matter and continue to follow his ambition.

Thinking back to the fun times they had had, she missed his quick wit but didn't miss the endless hours alone because he had other things to take care of before her. Understanding that starting up a business was difficult, if she ever chose to do that she knew she would have to work hard in the beginning but would ensure her husband was part of the business so they could work together. If he didn't want to do that kind of work, she would at least put aside time each day to spend with him. If love like that was not possible then a choice would have to be made on what was most important. For all she knew, Jeff had made this choice and decided to see multiple women and wasn't interested in a single relationship anymore. Well, it was not a problem now, so she shook her head to get the thought out of her mind and went up the stairs to get ready for work.

Emily really enjoyed her job, especially the creative part and designing what she wanted not what someone else directed done. Now that there was no one special in her life, the move to Paris was a serious consideration. She had met some designers and sellers from Europe, and one had even given a job offer after he had seen her work. He had scheduled a trip for her to go to Paris and look over the industry the very next month, and she had agreed gladly. Knowing what to look for, a decision would be made on what to do after the trip.

She finished getting ready and picked up the drawings she had completed the night before. The sketches were very imaginative, and she hoped that the new designs would be bought up quickly by the public and a new trend would be started. Young people especially got tired of the same design, and if the styles were accepted at all, she believed they would have an impact on the industry at least for a while.

Looking at the clock, she would have to hurry, so running down the steps her purse was grabbed quickly as she briskly walked out to the car. Jeff would be called later when there was a break in the day's activities.

Jeff arrived at the office and was surprised that Emily had not gotten back to him yet. Sitting down in his chair, the last few months went through his mind as he looked out of the window. Since Emily left, he hadn't been lonely. There were different ladies seen on different occasions, and they comforted him when he had a few minutes to relax. The time had gone by quite quickly, and there hadn't been enough time in the day to miss having someone at home when he got there at night.

Emily didn't know about the other women, and none of them meant anything to him. Whenever one of them was around, they satisfied his needs and gave him some company when he wanted it. Once they had gone home, he was fine with that too. Each one of them saw other people as well, so there really wasn't an issue with any serious relationship talk.

When one had gotten pregnant, he had offered some money and a contact he knew that could take care of the situation. At first he didn't think she wanted to go in that direction, but once he explained how it was for the best considering her future, she agreed and everything was taken care of. It had been that easy.

All of that was nothing Emily needed to hear about. Now he had to decide if he wanted to stay single and keep seeing multiple women or if he wanted to settle down with Emily. He hadn't felt as comfortable with any of the women he had been meeting as he always felt with her. Funny how he had given the other women little attention and they asked for little, but Emily demanded attention and to be treated certain ways. She was sure of herself and had confidence which is the reason she wouldn't be treated like the others he saw, and maybe that is what made her worth much more to him.

She always brightened his day, except of course when she kept harping about religion. He had plenty of time to take care of that part of his life once he had gotten into the position he wanted to be. He didn't care if she went to church or joined in the groups that banded together to study or perform volunteer services. Giving money to support the church was alright with him too, but he wasn't ready to join all of that. That would have to be made clear to her. If she agreed to those terms, then he wanted her back and they could get married. They would have to talk it through.

As he was looking out of the window, he noticed Brett's car was still not in the parking lot. His car had not been in its parking space when Jeff arrived, so he asked his secretary if she had heard from him. She had not, so Jeff decided to give him a little more time, and if he did not come in, someone would call him.

Emily called back and told him it would be fine to meet at their favorite restaurant that evening about eight. He agreed and smiled as he shut his phone off. Right after her call, the telephones started to ring, and the callers were from various foundations and organizations he had asked to contribute to the educational research and development projects. Jeff was confident and answered the different questions that were asked. Each caller asked for further information, and they were assured they would receive it by the next day. Once off of the phone, the list of what was needed to be put together for the investors was reviewed.

He was going over the requests as he walked to Brett's office. The designer was still not in, and the secretary said he had not called. His team was quite concerned because Brett rarely missed work. He did have a family, but he spent little time with them. Designing special projects such as the educational ones they were currently doing was his passion, and he didn't want to do anything else.

Steve, the second in line to Brett, came into the room and saw Jeff. "Sorry that Brett isn't here. Is there something that I can assist with?" Jeff asked the status of the projects, and the two began to go over the list he had been given by the potential benefactors with the timelines of when the materials were to be sent to the corresponding donors.

Jeff told Steve he was meeting a customer for lunch and would return that afternoon to continue the discussion. He would call Brett when he returned if the designer had not come in or contacted them. Walking out of the front door, the thought crossed his mind that the day off might have something to do with the discussion they had the night before.

The customer he met for lunch had many more questions than had been anticipated, and the meal took longer than expected. Jeff returned, and he and Steve continued the discussion on the options available. The phone in the assistant's office rang, so Jeff motioned to the secretary taking notes to answer and went on with the directions to Steve detailing when each layer of each project should be finished and ready to test. As they were speaking, Jeff glanced over and saw that the secretary was staring out the window while holding the phone. "What's the matter?" he asked her. Turning toward them, she let the two know that Brett's wife had been on the phone. Brett had died that morning from a stroke.

Jeff couldn't believe what the secretary had just said, so he asked her to get Brett's wife, Shelly, back on the line. The phone was handed to Jeff as soon as someone answered, and it was Brett's aunt who said Shelly was not available. She confirmed that his designer had died at the hospital that very morning. He had had an aortic aneurysm, and a small piece broke off and moved to his brain causing a stroke. Brett had lasted only a few hours because he wasn't strong enough to hang on. The doctor said he had checked Brett a month ago and his body was functioning well. The part of his brain affected would have been damaged, but many people survive that type of injury. The only thing the doctor could determine as to why his body was unable to even try to recover may have been caused by high blood pressure. His blood pressure may have been high from stress before the stroke and, of course, increased even higher as the stroke occurred. She had been told by his wife that Brett had been working very long hours and was concerned about his job lately.

Jeff was quiet for a minute and then asked if any arrangements had been decided on yet. The lady said that there would be a viewing the next evening at Benke's Funeral Home but wasn't certain if any of the other funeral arrangements had been completed yet.

He thanked her and hung up in total disbelief. How could someone who looked so healthy just disappear in an instant? Telling everyone to go home for the rest of the day in honor of their team member, he also told them the viewing day and time. Walking out to his car, an extra presentation Brett had left in his back seat came into view and tears slid down the sad face.

Composing himself after a few minutes, the short drive home began. He was not in the mood to do anything work related, so he called an old friend named Chuck to see how he was. Jeff had been thinking about Chuck lately and always remembered how his buddy used to make him laugh. With the nightmares and Brett dying, he could use some humor at this point. When his friend answered, he sounded great and they talked for quite a while.

Chuck was a certified public accountant and worked for charities in his spare time. He had been busy working the numbers for multiple construction projects to help the community's people in need, and there were so many requests, he told Jeff he could work seven days a week for years to come. The discussion changed to them both asking when they could get time off to go fishing together, and they both laughed when neither one of them could give an exact date.

When Jeff hung up, he felt much better and was glad that the call had been made to his college classmate. The world just seemed to be alright when the ones he loved and cared about were safe even if it was not the case for everyone. Smiling to himself, he looked at his watch and knew it was time to get cleaned up to meet Emily. First though, he had the business of calling back the donors to extend the timeframe to receive the information they requested. They were all very sad to hear that Brett had passed on, and each one agreed to wait for the data until the next week.

He arrived at the restaurant early still a little shaken over what had happened. The place was very full that night, and many laughing people enjoying their evening could be heard as soon as the front threshold was crossed.

Ignoring the noise all around, he stared at the table in front of him. Knocking the fork back and forth with two fingers, his mind floated from topic to topic until it settled on the bad dreams, and he suddenly wondered if any of the nightmares had anything to do with what happened to Brett. Somehow he felt that they were connected or were related in some way. Every time he closed his eyes, he saw himself lying on the floor dead instead of Brett. Maybe the dreams were just a warning that someone was going to die, but not necessarily him. He still couldn't understand the fiends that always appeared in the dreams or what their presence really meant.

Glancing up just in time to see Emily walk in, he stopped breathing for a moment as she appeared looking lovelier than he had ever seen her before. Clothed in a yellow dress, her hair gleamed and her cheeks glowed. None of the women he had dated lately matched her style or innocent beauty, and the relationships with the others made him feel dirty somehow. Emily would never live like the women he had been seeing. As he watched, she asked the maître d' where Jeff was sitting, and the man escorted her to the table where he was waiting for her. It was not lost on him that many men turned to watch Emily walk by.

He rose and held her chair for her, and then they just sat and looked at each other. The waiter appeared with water glasses asking if they would like to see the wine list. Jeff nodded, so the server left menus to be reviewed and turned quickly to retrieve the wine list of the week. Once the waiter left, Jeff didn't even glance at the menu, he was staring at Emily.

"What is the matter Jeff? You look terrible. Has something happened?"

"I don't know if you remember meeting our head designer Brett," Jeff looked at her. She nodded yes. "Well, he had a stroke today and died. He was only forty-five Em, and he has a wife and four kids." Jeff looked down at the table, and his hand started to shake.

"Is there anything that I can do?" she asked.

He shook his head and told her he had already talked to Brett's aunt. She said that Shelly had been very quiet and tearless, and that bothered him. "I wonder if she expected him to die. It sounds like she was preparing for this day and was just waiting for the incident to occur. I wonder if he had been sick but no one knew. Or maybe it just hasn't sunk in yet and the tears will come later."

Emily took his hand. He told her that there was life insurance through the company on each of the employees, so that would help Shelly with Brett's arrangements and help adjust from losing his income. "I don't believe there is a thing we can do. I'm not certain when the funeral will be, but the viewing is tomorrow night. Brett gave no indication that he felt bad or had any medical problems. I wonder if it had something to do with all of the hours he had been spending at the research lab. I feel bad about that, but it was his idea to put in so much time; I never asked him to put in that many hours."

He put his head in his hands. Somehow, Jeff felt responsible for his death or at least a contributor to it. The mortified objection Brett had over cutting the materials came into Jeff's mind and the guilt came back as well. He didn't mention any of that to his dining partner.

Emily felt bad for Brett's family and for Jeff too. "Jeff, he did what he loved, and how can that be a bad thing. I'm certain he loved his family, but his work is what made him thrive. He didn't know there were any health issues or he would have taken care of them. The thing I would want to know is if he was ready to die. Did he ever go back to church and begin practicing his religion again? He told me once he planned to and then begin a new way of leading his life. I hope he did just that. No one ever knows what is going to happen in the next minute, so this is a good reminder of what is important."

As she spoke to him, she noticed he was staring across the room at a wall. "Jeff, I hope that you have gotten ready in case something happens."

He didn't answer but looked at his glass.

She continued, "You know, if you don't feel like discussing our relationship tonight, I understand." She looked at him with sympathy, but he didn't appear to see her at all. She didn't know whether they should stay and order dinner or just leave and go home.

"Em," he began, "there is something else that is really upsetting besides Brett." He looked at her and then looked down. He did this several times and then told her about his nightmares. "I keep having these dreams. They begin where I am at a nice function, and all of a sudden I am thrown out into the street and inhuman beings are around me and talking to me. They have the shape of humans, but they are disfigured and almost look like something had tried to destroy them but they survived. They are horrible looking creatures with deformed features and sores all over, and they tell me that they are waiting for me. They assure me that I cannot escape. I'm not certain what that means or what type of event they are waiting for so they can take me. Now I think these dreams were a warning that someone was going to die, but not necessarily me. I feel bad about Brett, but I am so happy I wasn't the one."

The waiter came back to ask what wine they would like. Jeff chose a very nice vintage bottle and turned back to Emily. "Are you ready to order dinner yet?" Scanning over his menu, he noticed that Emily wasn't even browsing hers to see what was available.

"Didn't Jeff hear what he just said?" she thought to herself. She stared at him for a minute and he never even noticed she was distraught.

The waiter said he would be back in a few minutes to take their orders. Jeff finally decided on the house special and Emily just decided to have the same thing. The attendant returned, and after hearing their choices, told them it would be about half an hour for their selection to be complete. He suggested that they dance as the orchestra had begun to play.

Jeff didn't feel like dancing and didn't ask Emily if she wanted to dance. "We might as well discuss our plans for the future, Emily. We should get this settled and move on."

She looked at him and saw for the very first time that he really did not care one way or the other. Marrying her would just be something he did, but it wouldn't change him or how he lived. She didn't know if he saw other women, but it wouldn't matter, if he felt like doing that he would.

"What do you think," he looked at her. "Do you want to make another appointment with Fr. Lore and make our plans?"

She smiled and said, "You know that making arrangements with Fr. Lore will mean that you must go to Reconciliation before the wedding day so you can take Communion. It will also mean going to Mass once a week and to some special events during the week at times. I would like to volunteer with the St. Vincent de Paul organization, and both of us could maybe be lectors or ushers. We could even brush up on our knowledge of the Scriptures and teach catechism class. What do you think about that?"

"I will go to Confession and to church when I feel I can. I don't want to be forced into any of that, so if we make plans it has to be on my terms. I am very busy with the business and expanding sites, so I would think you would have a little consideration for that."

"That's just the point Jeff," Emily looked him squarely in the eye. "How do you know you will have time to do things on your terms? You must know some of the things you do are not right, so don't you pay attention to your conscience when something is wrong and you shouldn't be doing it?  Those are warnings Jeff.  I think you probably just ignore that voice inside of you and tell yourself you will take care of it when you have time?  You still don't understand that life on this earth is by God's terms, and when He calls, you will go ready or not.  If you are not ready, it is possible you will go to hell, and it is possible that the nightmares you have been having are a warning about you and you alone.  Did you consider that?"  He didn't flinch as she spoke.

"Well Jeff," she said, "I think you have given me the answer to my question.  You are not ready for a commitment, and you certainly are not ready to get married.  There really isn't any sense in us continuing this conversation.  I want a husband who enjoys me and is happy when children come.  I don't want a partner who is only concerned with making money.  So, I think our discussion is at an end.  I would love to be friends with you, and if you choose to, you can call me and keep in touch."  She patted his hand and looked into his eyes.

"Em, you aren't thinking at all about a future.  I understand what you are telling me about God.  I believe God comprehends the lives we live and that there are all different types of ways to exist.  People follow what they feel they must, and that doesn't necessarily mean they are ignoring God.  God understands, but you don't.  I am offering you a future that includes the good life; a life that has many good things to offer us for as long as we live."

She just looked at him for a minute, and then she chuckled and sat up completely straight in her chair, "No Jeff you are offering me a life that you want.  A life full of material things that you believe will create happiness ever after.  In reality, it will be a life full of devising more ways to make more money, searching for empty relationships so that high status can be achieved, and power grabbing to ensure you're at the top of the business world.  You will put yourself first always and then tell yourself that God understands you have to do what needs to be done on this earth to get what you want. His laws don't matter down here, and He will just invite you straight into Heaven because you did what you had to do. You believe He gave us laws to use if they fit into what we want, and so of course you can never offend Him. When you stand before God at judgement, you will just explain He is merciful and needs to understand that you had plans for your life. Others just didn't matter at the time, but when you are in Heaven you can do things His way. That is not what I want or what I will accept. I want something that is real for eternity." Emily smiled at him sadly, and he watched her stand up and slowly walk out of the restaurant.

"Well then it is finished," he thought. "I am not going to ask her back again. What does she mean by me getting ready for the end? I have a long way to go before I die, and by then, I will have made my peace with God. He understands much better than Emily thinks He does, and He knows that we have to do what we need to do on this earth. Of course He has Commandments, but they don't concern me now, and they are flexible depending on what era you live in. They have to be. She is never going to find a husband who will provide for her like I would with that attitude in this day and age, and I don't think I will ever forgive her for throwing away my offer. She was lucky I even considered her. Well I won't call her back or talk to her again ever."

He poured himself another glass of wine and sat back in his chair intending to relax and eat a nice meal. There was plenty of time to adjust his life, and he would do that someday. Until that point, God would understand and know he had to do what he had to do to make it in this world. He wanted power and money and would achieve both eventually.

Without any type of guilt, the last bite of the meal was eaten and the last of the wine was finished. Leaving the restaurant, he didn't feel like going home, so he drove over to his Uncle Ben's house. Sometimes he missed the old days when he worked for Ben and often now missed just seeing him. As he drove down the street to his Uncle's house, many memories came flooding back. Ben had taught him to throw a three point basketball so it went right into the hoop, Jeff was taught about the Catholic faith from him, and he learned how to treat people and talk to them while watching his Uncle run his organization. Ben had built a multi-million dollar business from a beginning in his garage, and he had a wonderful personality which drew people to him allowing him to click with most everyone he met.

As Jeff turned into Ben's driveway, he was happy to see the lights were on. Walking up to the door, the path was familiar and friendly giving a deep feeling of truly being home

The door opened just as he heard his Uncle say, "Look who's here!! My goodness I haven't seen you in months." The two gave each other a hug and Ben took him into the living room.

"Nothing has changed Uncle Ben; everything looks just like it did the last time I was here."

They both laughed and Ben went into the kitchen to get a couple of beers. Jeff heard the tabs pop on the drinks, and Ben appeared in the doorway, "Let's go out on the back porch. It is a beautiful night." The two sat on the same patio furniture Ben had had for at least fifteen years. Stretching out their legs, both looked up at the sky.

"I'm sorry it has taken me so long to come over here and visit, Ben. I started a business, and you know how it works with building up a company."

Ben looked over at Jeff and then back at the sky. "Lots of stars out tonight," Ben kept his gaze on the beautiful lights above them. "I know you have been busy Jeff. It does take a lot to get a business on its feet and finally start realizing a profit, but I did think you would be at your cousin Eloise's wedding. You shouldn't stay away from your family for so long, and you need to stay part of their lives.

Jeff gazed over at his Uncle as if he was being scolded. He played with the tab on the top of the beer can knowing Ben was right but not wanting to admit it.

"I also heard you were working with Ralph on some projects. Are you certain that is the path you should be taking? I have talked to several of the CEOs that fund your business, and they like you but are quite skeptical of Ralph having business with your research company."

"What did they say?" Jeff asked surprised. His shoulders went up around his ears certain that some of the dealings of the company were beginning to leak out somehow and there would be trouble. He knew the one thing Ben insisted on was honesty, and he certainly didn't want his Uncle to think badly of him. Ben had taught him that honesty truly made a good businessman, and using good judgement was necessary in any business deal. Of course Ben wanted to make a profit, but he would never do that by cheating someone else. In fact, several times his Uncle took a loss just to ensure everyone was happy with the transaction that occurred.

Ben didn't answer Jeff. He kept gazing at the stars, and then he finally broke the silence, "It doesn't matter what they say as long as you know you are doing what is right. People may not always agree with you, but if you are honest, people tend to take your word for things which creates a lasting bond with them. That is what makes a business successful, and that is what creates happiness. You know making money and working hard are fine, but it is making friends and helping and caring for others that make a person happy inside."

Jeff wanted to get off this subject, and he rummaged through his mind trying to find a topic that would bring some smiles and laughter to the conversation. After a few minutes of silence he said, "Have you been to that old movie house lately? One of my friends went there to see a show and said that they didn't even have popcorn. I guess the ceiling had been leaking, and all of the seats were wet in the first row he chose. What a mess! Remember when you used to take me there to see a movie. It was a palace then compared to now. We had lots of laughs watching those old shows."

He looked over at Ben remembering fondly the man who had been so good to him all of his life. When his father died, Ben had checked on his mother every night. He loved his sister and would do just about anything for her. Whatever broke down Ben would fix or have it fixed at no expense to his mother.

His Uncle would give him money and taught Jeff how to use the money wisely. Ben told him to take so much out for movies or fun and then save so much for something he wanted to buy in the future. Jeff knew he was very lucky to have someone like Ben in his life.

As Jeff reviewed the past, he noticed that Ben looked quite a bit older than the last time they had been together. His Uncle looked bent over, and his face looked worn with time. Funny that Jeff had never noticed that before. Ben had always looked tall and young to him even when Alice, his wife, had died. He thought back to when he had seen him last, and it had been almost a year earlier. Running into him at the grocery store, they had chatted for a few minutes, but he didn't recall noticing how much Ben had aged.

Glancing back at his beer, he knew nothing stayed the same, but he didn't feel any older. Why do people and times have to change so much, and why do they have to lose the people they love? Jeff began to feel odd and lonely as if he had already lost one of the best friends he had ever had. The visit lasted a little longer and then he told Ben that morning would come early so it was time to call it a night. They gave each other a bear hug and promised not to wait so long before the next visit. Jeff waved as he walked out to his car and felt very sad pulling out of that driveway.

His parents had tried to teach Jeff to think before making decisions, to work hard to get good grades and prepare for a career, and about the God they truly believed in. They never really disciplined him but instead gave heartfelt talks about mistakes and not making the same ones over again.

For Jeff, the discussions were boring and were ignored. As he grew older and became more headstrong the goal seemed to be making friends with troublemakers at school. This made him feel like part of something big and lead him to eventually get into trouble. His parents continuously stood beside him, and once he was caught stealing and his father talked to the store owner and got the charges dropped. Even that did not change his attitude or conduct, and Jeff continued rebelling into his college days.

Nothing his parents did ever made an impression on Jeff, and he just considered their effort something they had to do. He continued to get into conflicts ignoring the burden that was being put on them, and one night very unexpectedly his father died suddenly of a heart attack.

That is when his Uncle Ben took him under his wing. Ben made certain he stayed on the straight path and taught Jeff many good things about life including the fact that everyone was responsible for their own actions. Once in a while, the young man thought of his father and was afraid he had caused the heart attack by being a stubborn troublemaker and not listening to anything. Jeff began to listen to his Uncle and started to straighten out his life.

Ben became like a second father to Jeff and a best friend to his mother. Often the three went to church together, and his mother was very thankful that her brother took such an interest in her son and was even happier that Jeff seemed to respond to him. She watched as the two became closer and closer during the following years.

Eventually, Jeff began to work with Ben and would have taken over the business, but Jeff decided to change jobs for a woman who became a stranger. He had not done well at the new job, so he eventually decided to start his own educational research firm after talking to many people and learning about the gap that existed for different students. This new path was exciting to Jeff, and he truly felt a good impact on the world could be made.

The new business owner worked hard to find the right people to design what was needed and then to produce the products. The business was coming along, but as the organization grew, he learned that there was quite a bit of competition for funding in the educational research and development arena, and it was expensive to run the research firm.

Jeff thought often of the ethics Ben had taught him, but he reasoned that if he wasn't flexible, the business would never grow. He began to meet with organizations that could provide much needed funding, and he found himself stretching the truth to obtain financial assistance. Since working with Ralph, the business had really blossomed and had started to reap great profits. Jeff told himself he should stop working with an unethical person like his friend the advertiser, but the new ideas his partner came up with continuously helped to expand the business and increase the payoff. Besides, that is the way the world worked, and he had to survive in the world.

None of his family had been risk takers and had lived lives pinching pennies. The only one who did understand business was Ben, but his Uncle would never take the path that he took to gain profit. How Ben had grown his business and kept morals was a mystery to Jeff. He had not been able to accomplish that.

For a few minutes, he thought that maybe he really was on the wrong track in life. Maybe he wasn't meant to run a research firm or produce products to teach people. Maybe taking over Ben's business would have been a better course or something else altogether. He shrugged his shoulders and decided he liked the current plan and would continue on. He would be more careful in the future about the decisions he made, but the business had to be put first if it was going to make the kind of money and obtain the social status that became the final goal.

No thought was given to the goals that Ben might have had with his business when he began. His Uncle was very successful, very rich, and was invited to the finest social events. All of this and no dishonest actions were needed. No, Jeff didn't consider that at all.

It had been a long day and weariness seeped through his body. Pulling up to his garage door, the button wasn't pushed to open the door because he decided to leave the car outside. It was a beautiful night, and the stars were clusters in the sky. He breathed in the fresh air for a few minutes and watched the fireflies that were performing a light show. He enjoyed that and reminded himself to appreciate the surroundings more often.

Once inside, his wallet came out of the back pocket, and the phone came out of the shirt pocket. He had missed a call, so he listened to the message. It was Brett's wife, and the funeral would be held in three days. She was hoping that Jeff would speak about Brett at the church, and she would give him the details when he called her back.

Jeff started to think about Brett again. He had died so young, but had he been ready to die like Emily had mentioned? He was certain that Brett had been and knew God forgave and understood. What did God expect from everyone anyway? His thoughts said that he would be alright if what happened to Brett would happen to him, but deep inside he questioned that. He did not give God any time or go to church anymore, but he did believe that God existed in some form. Perhaps nature, maybe internally to each person's understanding, maybe just exactly as they spoke of God in church. Who really knew?

The next day, Jeff called Shelly and they discussed the arrangements. The viewing would be that night, the rosary would be the next night, and the funeral would be at one the following day. Jeff told her he would be glad to speak at the funeral and would have a prepared speech.

They hung up, and feeling the need to find a replacement for Brett as soon as possible, he called his assistant and told her in one week she should put an ad in the paper, on their business website, and also with the job finders they always used. It was really too soon after he died to consider going forward immediately to find someone, but he had to have a head designer. Brett's lead assistant was just not sharp enough to cover for him long. There were too many projects waiting in the queue, and they had to continue on immediately.

Jeff contacted some people in the business to see if anyone knew someone who would be a good fit for his opening. He got a few tips and contacted those he felt would benefit the company. Asking them a few questions, three of them seemed to be in line with what he was looking for. Appointments were set up for the following week so all of the business with Brett would be over and concentration could be put on the interviews. He would also make certain the details of each of the projects were included in the interviews to find out which of those being questioned were familiar with the concepts being produced to assist in hiring the correct person. If the interviews didn't work out well, hopefully the ads would produce some results.

That night at the viewing, Jeff walked in and saw Shelly and two of their older children speaking to people. Wanting to leave as soon as possible, he stood nearby and waited. As the other people moved away, he immediately walked over and took her hand and then gave a quick hug to each of the children. The sorrow on their faces showed how terribly sad and lost they were.

After discussing the rest of the arrangements with her, he asked if there was anything else they needed help with. She shook her head no and pointed out a few of the people who lived out of town and had come to help. A couple of minutes later the topics to discuss had been finished, so he gave her a brave smile and drifted off through the crowd so others could give their condolences.

He spoke with the people from the office and then quietly walked out and shuddered. He hated gatherings like this and never stayed any longer than necessary. He was not looking forward to the next couple of days.

As the priest started the rosary the next night, Jeff looked around to see if others were having a hard time remembering the decades of the prayer. Scanning the crowd, many were holding their rosary as if they carried and used it often, and they prayed with a passion that was surprising. Others seemed to say the prayer silently bowing their head. No one looked as if they were having problems following the priest.

After they finished, people gathered in groups to talk. Jeff went over to Shelly immediately to ask her how she was doing and if she needed anything. She looked tired and calm while telling him they were doing alright and there was nothing that they needed. Jeff touched her arm and told her he would see her the next day. Others started to approach Shelly, so he slowly walked to the door and left.

"Only one more day of this," he thought to himself walking quickly out to the car. He went directly home and turned on the television trying to forget the last few days. Flipping the channels, he found a show that looked quite interesting and decided to watch it until he was tired enough to go to bed. That didn't take long once he began to relax.

The next morning, Jeff got slowly out of bed and felt a great weight on his shoulders. Looking at the clock to see how late it was, he picked up the phone and called into the lab. "I won't be in until later on today because of Brett's funeral. Are many from the lab going?"

Brett's lead assistant had answered the call and told Jeff that everyone from the lab was planning on attending. He shouldn't worry though because after the funeral they were all going back to work.

That relieved Jeff a little, and they discussed the progress of the projects before hanging up. In the kitchen, he made some breakfast and just stared out of the window. He just didn't feel right about the day ahead. Sure, he was Brett's employer, but shouldn't someone in the family give the talk? Remembering Brett's kids' faces, sympathy swelled in his heart, and memories of losing his dad came back leaving a very sad feeling. The day ahead would be long.

Unenthusiastically going through bills laying on the desk, some old plans for new projects that had never started emerged from the pile. Maybe those would be of use some day, and he set them aside for a more thorough review later on. He looked at the clock and it was eleven. Needing to get ready and get to the church, he trotted up the stairs. In a few minutes, he came down, grabbed the few notes that had been jotted on a piece of paper, and walked out the door.

The comments written down sounded right and included nice remarks such as Brett's good nature, how he loved his family, and the work he had done that would change the way children learned for years.

Many mourners had already arrived, and he waved to some people standing in front of the church as the car turned into the parking lot. The people inside were sitting and standing, and Jeff found Shelly with a group of friends from the church. The casket was open for one last viewing before it would be closed for the final ceremony. She took him over to see Brett one last time, and then she left to say hello to a relative who had just arrived.

Jeff began talking to some of the people from the lab, and it only seemed like a few minutes before Shelly came up from behind and put her arm through his. "It is time to begin," she told him and steered him toward the front row. Jeff turned and saw that the casket had been closed.

The priest began the Mass, and after the homily, it was the main speaker's turn to address those gathered. Walking up to the podium fear seized the spokesman, but once started his apprehension was alleviated and full composure was regained. Jeff spoke well and gave their friend a heartfelt send off.

The tears from the crowd could be seen as the speech detailed the wonderful traits of the person who had left the lives of so many. Of course nothing would be the same, but the family had many great memories of the man who had been a husband and father to them. Friends and relatives had fond memories as well. The speech that ended with a simple prayer brought comfort to many.

Once the rite was over, all of the people from the research lab said goodbye to Brett's wife. Jeff told her he would call her soon and gave her his phone number again to make certain she could call him directly if she needed anything. Hugs and smiles were exchanged, and leaving the church he decided he wasn't in the mood to go home or go into the lab, so he stopped by a pub that was an old hangout to see if any of the old gang was there.

There were only a few people in there, and not knowing any of them, he sat in a booth toward the back and ordered a drink. The liquor tasted good, and slowly the anxiety began to disappear. He thought back over the day but never once considered all of the people he had seen at the funeral who had had their lives changed so dramatically by Brett's death. Besides his immediate family, Brett's parents and siblings had been there along with many other relatives. The only thing that Jeff focused on was the obligation to spend the afternoon at a memorial and talk about the deceased's life. Yes, he was sorry that his friend and designer was gone, but he didn't like funerals and didn't want to spend his time doing those things.

The waitress stopped back at the table and asked if he wanted another drink, and he did. Starting to feel much better, he thought back and wondered when the last time had been when he really felt that relaxed. Enjoying the time immensely, a decision was made to prolong it and stay there for several more hours. The day faded into the distant past, and the next day would be better. Letting out a long sigh of relief, a large tip was left, and there was no glance back as he walked out of the door.

He hadn't eaten since breakfast, so the fast food place ahead seemed inviting. He pulled into the drive through to order a meal off of the menu. Quickly the staff inside the food establishment had the order in a bag and handed out the window. The aroma was especially good that evening.

Once home, the suit was taken off and some sweatpants and a sweatshirt were pulled on. He flicked on the TV and sat down to devour the sandwich and fries that smelled so good. A comedy show was on, and for the first time in a long time, he sat there and laughed. He laughed so hard that tears were rolling down his cheeks, and as that show ended the next episode began. He felt the last bit of tension leave his body and decided to enjoy the feeling for a while. Around two in the morning, the tired, peaceful man started up the stairs to go to bed.

He flopped on the unmade bed sideways and went immediately to sleep. All of a sudden, he was back at Brett's funeral. The casket was outside, and the landscape around the area was beautiful with lush bushes and an array of flowers that smelled heavenly. He could hear music in the background and caught a glimpse of other mourners at a funeral down the path at another gravesite.

Standing by the casket absorbing the surroundings, it was apparent that the burial spot was a very peaceful place for Brett to spend eternity. Suddenly Jeff smiled because of a good memory of Brett and then walked closer to the box that held his friend. He bent over to look inside and saw himself. Stunned, he stood there not knowing what to do, and the casket started to sink into the ground. Jeff couldn't move but stood there watching the impossible. The box went lower and lower and he started to smell burning flesh. Blackened human limbs reached into the casket and began to claw and pull at him. His body began to move, and his eyes shot open. He looked up at himself and yelled for help as the creatures pulled him out of sight into the depths of what sounded like total despair.

Jeff was shaking all over, and he turned to run. Looking up, he saw a bright figure standing near. The shining form moved closer. "What did you see in that box?" the kind person said with a loving smile. "You have choices through your earthly journey, and only you can make those choices. You are the one who will realize joy or sorrow in this life and the next depending on what you choose. There is a time of ignorance and patience in the younger years, a time of promise to you when you gain faith, a time of the law as you understand what is required, and the end time of life as is currently known. What choices do you make with what has been given to you? You must be prepared minute by minute for the step from your current life into the next. Pray that you are allowed into glory."

Jeff blinked his eyes, and the form was gone. He began to wander around the burial ground and saw old markers move, and the people underneath stood up and said, "Welcome."

Screaming, he jumped out of bed running down the steps. Waking fully, he finally realized it had all been another awful nightmare, and as he stood on the steps in the dark the only thought was that the nightmares had to be dealt with.

"Maybe I should go to a psychiatrist," he thought still breathing heavily. "I don't know what is happening here, and I don't know who to talk to." He continued down the steps and went to the kitchen for a drink. His mouth was so dry he couldn't even swallow. Company would be nice, but the thought of calling one of the ladies he had been seeing was dismissed because they would never understand what he was talking about. Emily would understand, but she wasn't interested anymore.

Was all of this a warning sign, or was it just because of losing Brett and the impact of that? Why did he keep dreaming this type of horror, and in this nightmare, there had been a Heavenly person who was telling him to be prepared. Was he really being told that or was it because Emily was always harping to him about that? Was the nightmare derived from a mix of thoughts of Emily and their breakup and the funeral?

His head hurt from thinking, but sleep was not possible anymore that night. It didn't matter, because the thought of going back into that dream world was too upsetting. Pacing the floor, calmness finally started to come even though he was too upset to settle down completely. Attention had to be put on something else, so the television was clicked on for some company, and the newscaster gave the weather and then started on the daily news. Jeff listened as he continued to pace but stopped quickly as the newscaster said, "We have a special message for Jeff this morning from Hamartolos. The message is: Good morning Jeff. We enjoyed meeting you at the gravesite last night. Looking forward to really seeing you lowered into the ground."

Jeff turned instantly to look at the television, and blinking several times, all he saw was the newscaster reporting the daily news.

# CHAPTER SEVEN

He made an appointment with Fr. Lore the very next day and arrived a few minutes early at the church office. He wasn't certain how this conversation was going to go. Jeff hadn't been to church in years, and of course there was the issue with Emily. Well, something had to be done and this was all he could think of.

The office was silent that day, and not one person walked by on the street. The receptionist had let him in and then left for lunch. Within, the rattled nerves were settled a little with the surrounding peace and quiet, and he began to relax and collect his thoughts. Across the room hung a picture of the Lord with arms outstretched, and staring at it for a few minutes, he wondered why God couldn't be there to help out during this situation.

The door opened and Fr. Lore walked in with a bag of groceries. "Come on with me Jeff," he said. "We'll go over to the rectory and talk there." The priest walked briskly out of the door and down the walkway to the house he lived in. Jeff's pace quickened to keep up with him, and the priest fumbled for the keys as they approached the door. Inside, Fr. Lore motioned to the guest to sit at the kitchen table while the groceries were put away.

"Did you come to talk to me about the wedding? I haven't heard from Emily in a while, so I thought maybe you two had broken the engagement." He looked over at Jeff who was staring out of the window.

"No Father," he said. "I came to talk to you about something else. Emily and I have broken up; I thought for sure she would have told you."

Fr. Lore sat down across from Jeff and looked steadily into his face. The priest had been in such a rush, his visitor's bloodshot eyes, graying hair, and shaking hands went unnoticed at first. His face was taut and looked tired and upset, and his eyes had the gaze Fr. Lore knew so well of someone who didn't know what to do.

"Well tell me what has brought you here," he smiled at his guest.

Jeff gave a little smile and began, "I hope you don't think I am crazy Father. I've never heard of anyone going through this before, so please let me tell you all that has happened and maybe you can tell me what to do." He described all of the characters in the dreams and told the priest what had happened in each one. Every time the demons came up, Jeff started to shake and even had tears running down his cheeks at one point. Included was the bright vision of the shining figure and what the person had said. He sat still and waited for the priest to tell him what to do.

The room was deadly silent for a few minutes, and Jeff began to feel uncomfortable. Fr. Lore got up and went over to the stove where there was a tea kettle full of hot water. He poured himself a cup and plunked a teabag into it. Turning, he lifted the cup asking his guest if he wanted tea as well. The visitor shook his head no, and the priest began to speak.

"Jeff it sounds like your conscience is showing through in these dreams by frightening occurrences as if somehow you believe you deserve to be treated like this. The nightmares are taking you to the dark side of the spiritual world, and I don't know if you have been reading about or experiencing any type of activity concerning evil spirits that is bringing these figures out in the nightmares. Whatever it is, it is sticking in the back of your mind to come out when you sleep."

The visitor looked at Fr. Lore with disbelief, but the priest continued, "How long has it been since you have come to church or gone to Reconciliation? From the dreams, it sounds like you could use some spiritual assistance, and someone has tried apparently from the bright figure that you saw. The vivid shape could have been your guardian angel or Michael the Archangel. The grotesque figures you saw must be from the underworld and should not be taken lightly. Why they believe they can appear to you and tempt you to their side is a mystery as normally they coax and persuade in ways that are not seen and try to make humans believe the demon's ideas are the person's. I think you should begin to go to church and definitely go to Reconciliation. You should also pray to God for protection Jeff. I don't know exactly what any of the dreams mean, but you might want to consider your spiritual life and take this very seriously."

Jeff looked at the priest in amazement thinking the minister had been reading too many books. Fr. Lore looked at him patiently and said, "These have definitely been warnings. Who or what is doing this to capture your total attention will unfold I'm certain, and you will want to be prepared when they come for the last time. You must keep your wits about you to ensure you have the gumption to push them away and choose God if you are put to that test. Do not feed the nightmares somehow to keep them alive. Make certain you stand your ground on the good side. This may be something psychological as well, so it is possible that a psychiatrist could assist. Whatever you do Jeff, begin to pray and put God as a priority. No one can do that for you. This is a choice only you can make, and this choice should be made immediately."

The guest sat across from the priest with his mouth open. "You can't be serious Father. I know praying helps, but I am looking for a way to stop having nightmares that scare me to death. I don't think anything is really coming after me, but they are terrifying. I haven't done anything to bring this on. I live in the world just as you do, and so I participate in the world. God understands that we have to live on this earth. I was hoping for a prayer from you or something like that to ask God to make the nightmares stop."

The priest made the sign of the cross and the two bent their heads as a prayer was said. Once the petition to God was finished, the priest looked at his caller and added gently, "Whether these dreams are a warning or just an offspring of something from daily living, think carefully about your life. You can call me anytime you want to talk Jeff, so remember to contact me if you need to."

Jeff left the rectory upset and confused over what he should do. He knew Fr. Lore was serious, but he didn't feel as if the priest had given him anything he could use to get himself out of this situation. He thought about calling Emily but knew she would give him much of the same advice the priest had just given, and he was through with her anyway.

Getting into his car, the confused man began to drive around the city. Fr Lore meant well, but everything couldn't hinge on religion. There had to be a deeper reason for the nightmares, and maybe the reason for them would become apparent as time went on. If he became really desperate, he would make an appointment with a local psychiatrist. One way or the other, the issue had to be dealt with.

There was no place special to go, so he just drove and turned whenever the inclination came to mind. Finally, the driveway to his house was near, so driving to it the car was pulled in. He felt calmer but no closer to a solution. Then he thought, "I will just put all of my time into my business. I'll work so hard and so long each day that I will be too tired to think of any of this, and hopefully I'll be too tired to have a nightmare.

Across town, Fr. Lore was on his knees in the church before the holy Tabernacle asking God to help and protect Jeff. He didn't know what was happening, but whatever was causing Jeff's unrest, he knew God's assistance was needed. The priest finished his prayer and sat back in the pew thinking about the situation. So many people got lost, and they never really found their way. Many had come to him, and a few had straightened out their lives and were very happy serving their God. Others just got lost in the crowd and never discovered what they wanted, needed, or were meant for. Fr. Lore sat there feeling very helpless and then remembered that whenever he prayed for others, they were always touched somehow by God. The question was if they would respond to the grace given. The priest made a final sign of the cross and stood up to go back to the rectory.

The next day, Jeff put his plan into action. He worked constantly and took no time to relax or see friends and relatives. The calendar on his desk was full of meetings and lab testing, and of course he kept continuous communication open with the organizations that funded his projects. After a week, he felt more rested than in days previous to the schedule change.

Hard work was starting to pay off, and one morning Jeff woke up and stretched looking out of the window at the bright sunshine. He was excited and was hoping it would stay a beautiful day. Dressing quickly, he ran downstairs and made some quick toast. He wanted to get going early today because it was a big day for the business. Out the door he went and pulled out of the driveway with a smiling face. Yes, today was going to be a good day.

Stopping by the lab, several of the technicians who might be able to answer questions he couldn't climbed into the car. He drove quickly across town to the newest site he had opened in Orlando, and people who had been invited from the organizations that funded the research projects were collecting in the lobby. Two other sites for the business had opened in Orlando, and more had opened in a few other states as well in the last year. His business had grown tremendously, and new sites were not only launched across the country but planning was being accomplished to establish his business in foreign lands.

Jeff had replaced Brett with a designer who had great foresight, and they had worked together to create educational materials that he had not thought possible. The new productions were mind challenging, displayed excellent training techniques, and were produced in many languages. His contributors were excited about the expansion, and they truly liked the materials that were demonstrated for them. Hard copy, video, and audio all had a major place in the training plan.

Ralph had appeared at the old lab often and talked his partner into cutting the first version of the new training as well as the old. The reduction would create more disposable income to spend in other areas. Ralph told Jeff that they could update the packages in the future with the better methods and then resell them. The states and the countries that could afford to purchase the teaching aids would buy the first production and update as necessary. They would have the funds to do that. For the states or countries that could not afford it, their kids would benefit from the first version anyway. They shouldn't worry about the extent of what the people using the techniques or products could teach as the material still offered something for every child and it would be up to them to utilize what they had to the fullest.

The money from other countries could be sent through certain organizations that could move the funds and products ensuring the research company would lose less on tariffs and taxes. The world lay before them, the advertiser laughed, and there was no stopping how much money they could make.

For months Jeff worked such long hours he often had a hard time staying awake while driving home. He was not worried anymore about falling asleep and having a nightmare; in fact he began to forget about the dreams. There was no time in his life for such nonsense or to think about that part of the past anymore. He was doing well, and this was going to be status quo from this point forward. All of the plans that he and Ralph had made were being realized, and money was not the focal point during these days. All Jeff wanted to do now was to gain more power in the business world, so he pursued more contacts and as much open communication with his current funders as possible.

The people invited to view the latest site were impressed with the top of the line technology installed in the labs. Demonstrations were given of the new techniques utilized to develop and design the up and coming material for the new generation entering the educational arena.

When the function ended Ms. Trimble, a valuable resource of information, approached and asked Jeff to visit her office the next day. He agreed readily and told her he would be at her office around one.

That night, Jeff was ecstatic about how well everyone received the displays that had been presented. He was also intrigued with the prospect of meeting the one woman who loved to give out details of others' lives and actions. Although she was a hopeless gossip, she had provided a great deal of information about others that Jeff had used in the past.

The next day the outer office was empty when Jeff arrived, so he knocked on Trimble's office door. She told him to enter and asked him to take a seat. She was a nice, older lady with silver hair who always dressed in the finest of clothes and was always friendly and loved to chat. Taking a seat, Jeff asked if any word from corporate had come in about funding for the communication skill courses being designed for production.

Ms. Trimble had run the foundation office in Orlando for the corporation for years, and she knew just about everyone in the city and surrounding area. Her knowledge was not only about organizational business but included peoples' personal business as well. After telling Jeff that no word had come back yet concerning the funding, she began to talk about the city's leaders whose acquaintance could benefit her friend. They talked in length about several men in prominent positions, and she remarked on how Mr. Edmonds of the Chamber of

Commerce might be interested in helping Jeff become more involved in the political world.

As quickly as the wind can change direction, Ms. Trimble changed the subject and said, "Didn't Brett Jacobson work for you?" Jeff nodded and thought that it was quite odd to bring Brett up after all of this time. "Well," she continued, "isn't it a shame that that lovely wife he left behind killed herself?"

Jeff could not comprehend what she had just said, so he sat there motionless. Ms. Trimble rose from her chair and walked around to the front of her desk, "Please don't tell me you had not heard. Are you alright?" Jeff still said nothing, so she continued, "Yes, it seems she struggled with money matters for quite some time and it became too much for her. They found her body in a running car locked in her garage. I feel sorry for the children as they still are quite young you know." Then she changed the subject again and started talking about a young woman they both knew who she felt would make an excellent congressional candidate.

Forgetting everything but the business, he had neglected contacting Brett's widow to find out how their family was doing. Although Shelly had left a couple of messages on his phone, he never called her back or checked on them. When he did think of calling her back, he decided she had called too long ago for it to matter anymore.

Jeff tried to be polite and muttered a few words here and there but excused himself as quickly as possible. He walked through the lobby and out to the car stopping between his car and another to catch his breath. How could that have happened? Why hadn't he heard that it had happened? Stepping into his car, he called Brett's house, but no one answered. Maybe they just weren't home. Still upset, Jeff drove home, and after pacing the floor for some time got on the computer to pull up obituaries looking to see if this really had happened.

He went through page after page and then stopped with a jerk. There she was. He read the obituary and learned that she was only thirty-five years old. Their children were eight, ten, twelve and thirteen. No other information was given, so he went back to the paper to try and find the story. It had been just as Ms. Trimble said. Jeff shut the computer off slowly and stared at the wall.

"Why hadn't he called her? If he had called her, maybe he could have given her money and this would never have happened. Maybe she had just needed someone to talk to." He put the palm of his hands over his eyes.

In just a few minutes, the normal voice of excuse whirled in his mind. "I can't track everyone and take care of myself and my business too. They have family members that should have been looking in on her; not a stranger. I can't take responsibility for this, so I'm not going to worry about it. I'm certain the grandparents or aunts and uncles will take the kids, and everything will be fine."

Walking into the bathroom, he decided firmly he was right. He would have to concentrate on his life, and everything would work out. He pushed the thought of Brett's wife from his mind and trotted down the stairs. The subject would not be revisited in the future. All that could be done was, and there was nothing else to be said.

He began to think of Emily and how she would react to the decision. That thought was dismissed too as it didn't matter what she would think. She was out of his life.

Looking at the clock, he grabbed the suit jacket hanging on the back of a dining room chair and went out to the car. The vehicle's window was open, and the air smelled fresh as he drove slowly down to the lab to see what was going on.

The receptionist at the front desk said hello and then handed him a package. Jeff glanced at her quickly with a questioning look, and she told him a man had stopped by and said that this research lab and the other sites as well were going to be investigated. He was from the Federal Trade Commission, and his business card was in the package. The visitor told her that the agenda was detailed inside, and the investigator would be back the following day at ten o'clock to begin. Jeff was to be there and be ready to answer any questions that may come up. Records would also be needed for at least the last three years.

Jeff picked up the large envelope and went into his office without looking back or thanking the front desk assistant. Fingering the envelope but afraid to open it, the phone was picked up and Ralph's number was dialed. After telling the advertiser what had happened, Ralph asked, "What does the paperwork say?"

"I don't know; I haven't read it yet. Why would they be investigating my business? Someone must have called them and complained, but whom? How am I going to explain all of the amounts on the bills and the quantities? How are we going to answer questions about our expenses on our records? I thought no one ever looked at the individual documents only the totals in the financial report. What if someone is complaining that the materials aren't what were offered?" Jeff said very upset, and then he waited for a reply.

"Just calm down," Ralph told him. "I will come over tonight and we will go over the books. Tomorrow, I will send my accountant and lawyer over to sit through the meeting with you. They will know how to answer this joker's questions, and maybe they can get rid of him for you tomorrow."

Jeff was very quiet for a minute and then his voice became almost inaudible, "I hope so, because this was your idea." He hung up and started to pace around the room. Why had he listened to Ralph? He should have known that if something bad happened, he would have no solid proof that Ralph was involved, and he would take the blame for everything.  All of the money was paid under the table to Ralph in cash.  Why had he been so stupid?

Well, maybe Ralph's accountant and lawyer would get this guy off of his back.  They were experts, and they could at least tell Jeff what to do after the meeting was over.  Besides, his partner wouldn't want to lose the money that was continuously put in his pocket from their alliance.

But no matter what Jeff told himself, there was no settling down.  He started to sweat and felt a wave of sickness traveling from his throat to his stomach.  A pain started in his chest and worked its way to his shoulder.  This started to frighten him, so he sat down and tried to breathe slowly and quietly.  Reaching over to pour a glass of water from the pitcher on the desk, he suddenly slumped to the floor.

# CHAPTER EIGHT

After the ambulance left with Jeff, the secretary called Ben whose name was listed as the next of kin. "Hello, Mr. Case?"

"Yes, this is he," Ben answered.

"Hello, I am Cindy from Jeff's office. Jeff was just taken by ambulance to Forrester Hospital. He has you listed as his closest relative, so I wanted to let you know as soon as possible."

"Did they say what was wrong?" Ben asked very concerned.

"No, they didn't Mr. Case. I'm sorry. The first responders were busy trying to revive your nephew. I think you should probably leave for the hospital as soon as you can."

"Thank you," he said as he put the phone down. He tried to settle his nerves and think of exactly what he should take with him to the hospital. Jeff had spoken to him about this type of situation, and Ben knew that he had a power of attorney for health care that Jeff had made out and signed just in case something like this should happen. He went into his office to get it, and looking across the desk, his eyes caught the picture of him and Jeff on the last fishing trip that they had taken together four years earlier. Ben stopped and studied the picture for a minute and then sighed deeply. He thought about how quickly his wife had died and how no one knows from day to day what might happen. He grabbed the document and walked out to his car not even noticing his neighbor wave to him as he pulled out.

Ben parked in the large lot of the hospital aware that he might be there for some time. Once he got to the front information desk, he asked where to find Jeff. A pleasant volunteer put Jeff's name into the computer, and as the information came up, she softly told Ben that he was in the intensive care unit. She gave him directions to get to that part of the hospital, and after thanking her he turned abruptly and started down the long hallway.

The elevator took a long time at each floor as there were many people waiting. It was late afternoon, so the hospital was quite busy, but Ben was stunned and didn't notice anything. He waited patiently, and reaching the fourth floor he turned right from the elevator doors as the lady at the information desk had told him. He saw the nurse's station and went to the first nurse who appeared, "Hi, I'm Ben Case, and I've been called up here for Jeff Bellows."

The nurse smiled at him and went to her computer. After finding Jeff's name and reading the synopsis of the case, she told Ben that she would call the patient's doctor. If he would please take a seat in the waiting room to the left, the doctor would be in as soon as he finished with his current patient.

Ben gave the nurse a nod and went to the waiting room. There was a woman pacing the floor, and she didn't even see him as he entered. Another couple sat at the far end of the room trying to concentrate on the television newscaster. Ben didn't know what to do, so he sat down and watched the window on the door hoping the doctor would walk in. Without realizing it, Ben had folded the power of attorney and kept creasing the paper over and over again. Trying to breathe quietly, the waiting and unknown diagnosis that was coming made the time stand still. He didn't know how long he sat in the chair but no movement was made until the doctor finally walked in.

'Hello Mr. Case, I'm Dr. Jasper. Please, let's go into my office and we can discuss your nephew's case." The doctor showed Ben to his office and closed the door. "I am sorry to have to tell you that your nephew suffered a massive heart attack. The damage that has been done is severe, and I am afraid that the prognosis isn't good. We have Jeff on life support, and he is comfortable. He can breathe on his own at this time, but we are taking precautions incase this function cannot sustain itself and then the machine will take over. We don't know how long really the brain was deprived of oxygen, but we feel that massive brain damage has occurred. Of course, we will continue to work with Jeff until we have reason to believe that our care will no longer benefit him. Do you have any type of legal document giving you the power to determine Jeff's care in case he cannot speak for himself?"

Ben sat and listened in disbelief as the doctor spoke. Then he looked the doctor in the eye and said, "He is only forty-one years old! How could this happen? He is in good shape and is constantly on the move."

"I know," the doctor said. "Jeff has an abnormality in his heart. I'm certain he has been to the doctor before, but sometimes these imperfections are hidden and not easily found. Unfortunately, I believe he had some type of warning signal but ignored it. That happens frequently, especially when someone is Jeff's age. This is terrible news to have to tell you Mr. Case, but you really do need to think about what Jeff would want you to do if his condition deteriorates. We will help you anyway we can, but some hard decisions will more than likely have to be made."

Ben asked if he could see Jeff, and the doctor told him he would let the nurse know and she would be in to get Ben as soon as possible. The doctor stood, squeezed his shoulder, and walked him back to the waiting room. Ben stared at the floor unable to move. He loved Jeff like a son, and then he thought of his sister. He had loved her dearly too, and she had died some time ago. Losing Jeff was hard to think about, but believing he would meet his mother in Heaven softened the blow. Why things like this had to happen wasn't understood, but he had faith in God and wiped the tears from his eyes. His faith told him that people had to trust that God knows what He is doing. Ben believed that good always came from bad even if one really never found out the positive side.

As he looked around, there was no one else there, and he was alone in the room of fear where many people sit waiting for the news that their lives have changed forever. It seemed like hours before the nurse came into the waiting room to get him. When she entered, she smiled and motioned for him to follow her. They went around two corners and then stopped in front of a closed door. She pushed the door open and smiled as he began to walk in.

The room was dim and very quiet. The only sounds that Ben could hear were the machines doing their job as they monitored and assisted where needed. It seemed to him that Jeff was hooked up to every imaginable type of equipment, and he stood there hoping Jeff would open his eyes. Touching his nephew's arm to let him know that he was there, the visitor looked Jeff's face over carefully and noticed it was ashen in color and his breathing was very shallow.

After a few minutes, Ben walked over to a chair and pushed it to the side of the bed. Sitting down, he stayed in the patient's room all night. Every few hours he got up to pace back and forth to calm his nerves, and then he sat back down and stared at the tubes, machines, and the walls. He could still hardly believe that his nephew was this sick. Jeff had been at his house only a few weeks before laughing and talking old times.

In the very early hours of the morning, Ben drifted off to sleep in the chair. He had made it most of the night but was too tired to think anymore. Only an hour after he had fallen asleep, the door opened slightly and a lady looked in. She had tears in her eyes, and she quietly walked over to Ben. When she saw he was resting, she went to the other side of the bed to see Jeff.

Emily had been caught totally unaware when a nurse at Forrester Hospital called her. Emily and Cheryl had been friends for a long time, and Cheryl knew all about her engagement to Jeff and how it had ended. The nurse knew her friend would want to know that Jeff was in the hospital, but she didn't tell Emily any information about what had happened or how sick Jeff was.

Thanking Cheryl for the information, they hung up, and she called the hospital to see if they could ring Jeff's room so she could talk to him and see if there was anything he needed. The caller was very surprised when they told her he was in the intensive care unit and only family members were allowed. There were no telephones in the room, and the person at the desk had no information they could give her.

She dressed hurriedly and called into work leaving a message telling them what had happened and that she would be late coming in. Saying a quick prayer for Jeff she went out to the car hoping for the best. Had it been an automobile accident, had he fallen, or was he sick with a virus? She drove to the hospital telling herself that he would be alright, and once it was in sight, she called Cheryl on her telephone to ask what floor and room Jeff was in so she could go directly there and bypass issues at the front desk. Cheryl looked it up quickly and told her friend how to get there and then called the intensive care unit desk to see if she could get Emily through without a problem.

Once on the floor, the visitor started to search for the room. Finding it, she looked around quickly to see if anyone was going to stop her, and as no one was in sight, she slipped through the entrance. The dim room and silence kept her leaning against the door for a few minutes until she could grasp her surroundings.

As she stood above Jeff, her heart felt broken. Even though they had agreed their relationship was ended and had parted, she had always hoped that Jeff would change his mind about the course of his life and they would one day get back together. Maybe they still would.

Carefully sitting on the edge of the bed, she began to pray for him. After a few minutes, she thought about Fr. Lore and wondered if the priest had been called. Deciding the call must be made immediately, she stood to leave the room just as Ben woke up and saw her.

"I'm glad you are here," he gave her a hug. Ben told Emily everything the doctor had said, and then Emily asked him if the priest had been called. "I didn't even think of that last night regretfully. I will go and call Fr. Lore now and get out of this room for a few minutes."

Emily sat down in the chair Ben vacated and thought about the first time she had met him. Jeff had taken her to a wedding reception, and Ben sat at their table all night. She was very touched about how close Jeff and his Uncle were, and she and the older man had hit it off immediately. The next day, Jeff told her all about Ben and how his Uncle had been there for him his whole life. Beginning to pray again, God was thanked that such a kind man was there.

After a few minutes, the visitor got up and walked slowly to the window. She knew the outcome would be up to God, and she wondered if Jeff had taken her advice and talked to Fr. Lore before this happened.

Ben came back in the room with some coffee and sat on the edge of Jeff's bed facing Emily. The coffee tasted good, and it warmed the room a little. Suddenly, the alarm on one of Jeff's machine's started to blare. A nurse appeared immediately to check the status of his vitals, and Ben and Emily moved out of the way.

Once the nurse was satisfied that everything was alright, she turned to the two watching her and asked them if they were relatives of Jeff's. Ben told her who they were, and he made certain to tell the nurse Emily was his fiancée. The nurse smiled and told them that the patient's condition had not changed since they brought him in, so if they wanted to go to the cafeteria and take a break it would be fine. They thanked her and left to go to the lower floor.

"Fr. Lore is on his way up," Ben told her. "He was surprised to hear that Jeff is so ill and wants to make certain that he is given the Sacrament for the Sick." Emily got tears in her eyes again and patted his hand. She knew that Jeff was the last living relative Ben had and knew this was very hard on him.

They both had a bagel and ate in silence. Neither one wanted to go back to that room, but neither one could stay away either. What if his condition deteriorated while they were gone? Slowly, they walked to the elevator and went back to the floor where the one they loved was. Fr. Lore had already arrived and was giving Jeff the rite for the sick.

"Hello," the priest said to both of them when he was finished. "I am so glad that you called me; I had no idea Jeff was here and was so seriously ill."

"Have you seen the doctor come in?" Ben asked him.

"No, no one has been in here since I arrived. I would like to wait with you until he does come to check on Jeff."

Just then, the door opened and the doctor with a team of other doctors and interns came into the room. The physician nodded to the visitors and proceeded to the bed. He read the chart telling Jeff's vitals throughout the night and began his routine visual checks of the patient's condition. For a few minutes he spoke to the group he was with in medical terms that were foreign to the visiting observers. Several interns asked questions, and then the group left the room leaving the doctor to speak to the family members.

He introduced himself to Emily and Fr. Lore and then began to tell them about the patient's condition. "Jeff seems to have had a quiet night as his brain waves have been steady. His pulse and blood pressure have been high at times, and other times almost normal. This can be caused from various things, but nothing so dramatic that we have concerns at this time. His heartbeat is fluttery, and his

103

temperature seems to be rising which could be an early indication of an infection. We are going to bring other pieces of equipment into the room today to repeat tests, and we will also be taking new x-rays to ensure the heart is not enlarging. After we get these new results, we will see if there is anything further we need to do or if we just need to wait for Jeff. Does anyone have any questions?"

Emily asked when Jeff might wake up, and the doctor told her he couldn't answer that. That was one thing they would have to wait for Jeff to do on his own. With no other questions to answer, the doctor said goodbye and left the room.

The two looked at each other and then the priest. Fr. Lore spoke to them for a few minutes and then had to leave for an appointment. He assured them he would be back that evening before walking out of the door, and the two returned to their chairs. The monitors on the machines hooked up to the patient still beeped and clicked in a synchronized way. It was almost hypnotizing for them to watch the movement of the lines waiting for something to suddenly happen.

After several hours of watching, Ben stood up, "Do you plan to stay with Jeff too until he is out of the woods?" Emily nodded yes and her eyes filled with tears again. "Alright," Ben said, "then let's do this in a smart way. We can take shifts. I'm free twenty-four hours a day, so maybe it would be better if I stay during the day while you have to work, and then you could go home and get some sleep and come back here later in the evening to stay with Jeff so I can have a break. Does that sound alright to you?"

Emily nodded again, "Yes, that is fine, but you have been here a long time. Go home and get some rest, and we can begin our new schedule tomorrow. If you could come back by six in the morning, I could go home and get ready to go to work. I can do that every day for a while, and then he won't be alone and you won't spend all day and night here."

Ben nodded and went by the bed one more time. He took Jeff's hand and held it and stroked the patient's cheek. After a few minutes, he turned and told Emily he couldn't leave. Ben went back to the chair and decided he would stay until Jeff woke up.

She nodded and moved to the bed picking up Jeff's hand and patting it. "Maybe you will come back to me," she said softly to him. She stared out of the window, and gazing at the wide sky asked silently that Jeff be taken to Heaven if he had to leave.

# CHAPTER NINE

At that very moment, no one knew that Jeff was in his last hour of earthly life. There were no outside indications that the end was near, and the monitors showed the same vital stats that had been shown all along. He appeared to be sleeping peacefully making no movement or sound, and anyone looking at the patient would have expected him to come around at any time and continue on as usual.

Behind the eyes that were closed, Jeff was wide awake. He found himself walking along a path on the side of a mountain with a soft breeze blowing in his face. The ocean was on the left, and great waves were thrashing the rocks around its shore while an old fishing boat was out on the water with men throwing nets into the sea. Glancing upward towards the warm sun, a beautiful blue reflected a splendor only the sky can give.

Suddenly and for no particular reason, thoughts went rushing through his mind of the life he had lived so far. Events and actions that would be changed if they could be were seen mentally, but memories of victories appeared as well. The accomplishments of owning a business that generated millions of dollars a year and the power and status gained came to mind.

Smiling inwardly, he determined that life was going well, but a voice asked, "Have you looked back at how you treated others? Are you sorry for all the wrongs you have done to others and to God?"

Jeff was caught off guard with the questions that generated through his mind and began thinking about what he thought he had just asked himself. There were a few times remembered when something was said or an action taken that hurt someone that he wished could be changed, but those were minor occurrences and he didn't feel any of those things would alter his decisions about most of the things that had been done. The justification process used for everything still seemed appropriate.

Thinking he knew himself very well, he liked the way life was going and the choices that had been made. A few people in his life had talked to him several times about his attitude of hurting others in various ways with no apparent conscience, but the comments had been dismissed as either old fashioned or generated from jealousy. No, he concluded, he was living, acting, and making decisions as he always had and always would. His behavior was no different than anyone else's who would be doing what they had to in a world that cared about no one.

This line of thinking was not interesting to him, so he shrugged it off and continued down the path to see where it led. The type of moral reasoning that had just occurred had always bored and confused Jeff. Considering himself a realist and a modern type man, analyzing past mistakes and consequences had never been intriguing, and he did not intend to second guess himself and change his belief system on living to accomplish the goals that had been made. Delving into right and wrong often baffled him, but he always came up with an answer that satisfied what he was trying to do. The blame went to others when the outcome was not favorable, but when the result was what was desired, any consequences were for others to bear. The decisions made focused only on the conclusion that was best for his future, and he did things his way whether others liked it or not.

As he walked along, the wind acted as if it was becoming angry and began to whirl around him. The sea's waves became higher and higher. Wondering why the surroundings were becoming violent, he stopped and gazed out over the water and then towards the sky to see if a storm was brewing. He became quite perplexed when he saw that the sky above was clear and luminous.

The strolling continued, and suddenly he found himself walking into a strange land; a type of place he did not remember ever being in before. The sea had disappeared and there were trees and bushes all around. They seemed to move to different locations as he walked ahead, and as they moved, the path he was on shifted directing the trail to the horizon and almost nudging him along the way. He didn't understand how they changed position when they were rooted to the ground.

The trees and bushes vibrated emitting electrical pulses, and every plant version responded to the others' waves and tempos through their own communication techniques. Each growth around him displayed different characteristics. One bush had flowers, and one of the blooms lifted its satin petals upward growling and then howled. Down the path, a second one responded with cries and whines of its own. Another shrub had tiny spears all over each branch, and when Jeff reached out to touch it, the fingers were pulled back just before the stabbing motions of the plant were able to connect. He found a different plant appearing to be an herb that sent out a sweet smell and sang softly. Many others came into view as he strolled along; one with teeth that bit and chewed at those next to it, another that yelled in a strange language at the plant behind it and then started to pull it out by its roots, and one other that looked beautiful but burned whatever touched it.

Amazed by the few soothing plants mixed in with the multitude of aggressive varieties, the guest in the abnormal domain gazed up at trees with fruit wondering what they did. Far ahead and unnoticed before, the visitor squinted curiously at a lone tree near the horizon with hand sized leaves.

He observed that there were no buildings, cars, or roads, and no noises from any type of human activity that normally could be seen and heard. No animals scampered around, and no pets on leashes walked by attached to their owners' arms. He wondered where everyone else was and how he had wandered into this peculiar environment.

The air had a filmy gray color to it, and especially the few, calm and blissful bushes were covered with a thick see-through gray haze. How strange everything looked, particularly the horizon. Where the sky and earth met, it was as gray as the overcast surroundings he walked through, and there was no color or beauty in the earth and atmosphere that could be seen. How erratic the new surroundings appeared to be.

All of a sudden, the entire area seemed extremely isolated and void with an emptiness so great that he had never experienced such lonesomeness before. It felt as if he was totally empty inside and incapable of ever feeling joy within again. Stunned by the excruciating self-loss, Jeff began to consider where he really was.

Looking down, he noticed the path was an array of pictures. Not recognizing anything at first, he began to observe the way the representations were an integral part of the foundation of the corridor yet each three dimensional depiction stood apart from the trail. Each space spoke of an occurrence as if it were retelling a piece of a story as it led towards the horizon.

Unexpectedly, the path began to rotate first horizontally and then vertically under his feet, but the movement allowed walking without disturbing his steps. Watching closely, he began to understand that each one of these pictures was a piece of something he had experienced in his life. As the rotations took place, the pieces blended together to tell a story from a segment of previous years.

The slide at his elementary school appeared in one space, and as the turning continued, the entire playground scene from that fragment of history was shown. As the path revolved, he saw his first car, senior high school prom, and the old driveway where he used to play basketball. Continuing along, human figures came into view in each illustration. Stunned, he bent closer to the passageway and saw that the representations he remembered as being sad or recalled a bad memory were all intact. The depictions that made him feel happy or overjoyed had portions fading away as if the parts he wanted to retain were slowly leaving forever.

Looking around thinking bad lighting was causing some parts to appear as if they were vanishing, Jeff observed a darkly dressed person who had abruptly appeared and was standing in the middle of the path between him and the horizon. Surprised at seeing someone, he peered around and on the right side saw figures dressed in white who were bowing their heads. On the left, dark and gloomy figures stood just waiting. Waiting for what Jeff didn't know, but he felt very uncomfortable.

Perceiving that someone was speaking to him from the right, Jeff turned his head, but he saw no one talking. The voice said, "Ask for forgiveness." Not understanding why someone would say that to him and stunned by the interaction, he just stared and couldn't comprehend what the people on the sidelines were there for or what they wanted.

Still moving along the trail and approaching the tall figure, he saw that the man looked very prideful and arrogant. Dressed as if going to a ball, every bit of clothing the fellow had on was black, his grooming was impeccable, and superiority seeped off of him as he looked down at the naïve person headed his way. The black hair was cut very short, and odd looking jewelry with symbols adorned two fingers, shirt sleeve cuffs, and wrists. His eyes were almost slits, and for a second they looked yellow with small, diamond shaped black pupils. The man blinked quickly and Jeff saw that the eyes were actually black.

No smile showed on the stranger's face, but the eyes penetrated to the very center of Jeff's soul as the man inspected him from head to foot. The aura flowing out from the figure produced fear in the simple stranger who was approaching. Staring at the visitor with disdain, when Jeff was almost to him, he lifted his left hand part way and the pathway stopped.

The peculiar vision in front of Jeff began to speak very flippantly, "We have been expecting you. I see you have noticed quite a bit about your surroundings. The color of this special environment is from the atmosphere you continuously created for many others along your earthly life's journey. The plants reflect the decisions that you made, and the trees shed tears from their fruit for you. The same type of trees that watched another suffer greatly." The gloomy man threw his head back laughing and then continued. "The individuals on both sides have specific wishes for you. Those on the right were sent to assist, but they cannot help you, and nothing they do will make a difference. You have chosen to see nothing but the material things around you, and rightly so. We have worked hard to ensure you focused on the important things and that you were comfortable and well taken care of. Your pride has increased appropriately from the condition you were cloaked with at birth and has permeated each day of your life. The choices you have made have been very well received by us. This journey is different for everyone who comes, but for you it will be uncomplicated as we know what your choice will be, and that will lead to only one possible outcome. Continue to observe and enjoy. After this hour your earthly life will pass away and your mortal eyes will see no more."

Jeff was confused and couldn't believe what the man had said. He hadn't done anything that this stranger would know about. Sure he was responsible for taking charge of his own life and succeeding because no one else would do that. Thinking that judgement would come for the things that must be done in the only life he knew never really made sense. As a kid he had heard those at Mass and his parents talking about preparing for eternal life and of course there was Emily and Fr. Lore, but he had never bought into it. He believed there was a God, but He wasn't going to come down and run his life.

Immediately upon the man's departure, he had to admit to himself that something was happening. It felt like a dream or a nightmare, but the realization that he was actually in this place took hold. Jeff gasped as comprehension sunk in that he was dying and was here to receive judgement for his life.

The words from the stranger began to travel deep into Jeff's soul making him feel uneasy and then alone and hopeless. Memories of the past and times and things he did that hurt others, deprived others, and offended others flowed through his mind. Knowing the choice that had been made to ignore God and His laws sent a shiver down Jeff's spine, but he knew that choices were made on what was best at the time. Maybe he had chosen to take actions in his favor instead of others, but so did everyone else. God certainly would understand what he needed during his worldly life and not hold anything against him. God's laws were for church activities, and He would understand that Jeff couldn't follow them in the real world.

A figure from the left began to laugh, "You are right not to care about God or people." The thing took its thin, boney hand and scanned to the left. "All of us have assisted you with making the choices you made. Why shouldn't you want for yourself above others, and we made certain your thoughts justified the paths you took to gain what you wanted. Do you remember inner voices telling you to take care of yourself first? It wasn't hard to help you decide on our way. Now, you will join us, and we will enjoy each day." It laughed loudly and wickedly.

Jeff peered through the gray mist to see who was talking to him. The motions and movements of the being could be seen, but the thing was blurry and he couldn't get a clear look at it. Not understanding what was talking to him, he turned away from it missing the fact that it was one of the demons that had been in his nightmares.

"Enough," the tall man reappeared. "We will have eternity for this type of banter." The man did not want Jeff to recognize it as the vision might immediately cause the prey to beg for forgiveness and in turn allow him to be saved from the demons' grasp. He looked at Jeff and his left eyebrow arched, "Continue on."

Abruptly, the trees and plants moved apart and showed a much broader path. The pictures moved until the first entire scene came into view. It showed his mother and father crying in their bedroom and talking about how they had failed and why their son would break the law and not regret it.

He remembered the incident and talking back to his father. Jeff felt shamed but at the same time justified his actions as being young and unthinking. At that age he thought that he knew everything and his father was just an old man out of touch with the times. His father had given him a heart to heart talk about the importance of decisions as a person goes through life. Jeff had totally ignored the discussion and done as he pleased which lead to his arrest and being taken to the police station for stealing boots. His father had come down to the station to get him out, and Jeff never apologized once even though his father talked to the store owner and convinced the man to drop all of the charges.

The incident had upset his mother as well, but he just hadn't cared. In fact until this moment he never gave it a second thought. His parents had been good role models and religious people who had taken him to Mass every week, but nothing had touched Jeff's heart. His focus had been on girls and the friends that he saw at church not what the priest was saying. Now, it hurt him that his parents were so upset, but neither one had brought up the subject again.

Jeff stood there wondering why nothing of the incident had ever registered as important. No thought of how his parents were hurt was felt before, and never had he grasped how refusing to see things as they really were continued to affect his life.

"Well," he thought, "everyone does that type of thing. I suppose I shouldn't have talked like that, but they knew I was just young and immature.

A voice from the right said, "Ask for forgiveness."

Immediately a shadow from the left spoke, "Ask for nothing because you did nothing wrong."

Jeff was confused but confident that he really hadn't done anything mean enough to ask for pardon. He said nothing and just stood gazing at the shape when he felt something dripping on his head. Looking up he observed the trees with their tops bent down as if they were bowing. The leaves on the branches were wiping the tears streaming down from the small, oblong fruit. The branches on both sides of each tree came together as if they were hands and the trees were praying.

Staring at the unbelievable actions of the trees, his peripheral vision caught the movement and color changes on the floor. His gaze fell downward and the next episode appeared as the path moved in a circle.

The next scene was one of him with friends from college who liked to cause trouble. At the time, he thought it was pretty clever when they were able to intimidate others, and Jeff got an attitude just like his friends had. He liked being part of the clique, and standing by one night while the group leader raped a student from another college had not disturbed him. Jeff had had nothing to do with it, but he didn't try to stop it either. When the girl's parents called the police, the investigator had questioned the whole gang. Jeff felt torn about what to do, but he was part of the group and chose to lie about where they had been on that day at that time. The leader had not been charged.

The scene then changed to the girl's life and how that night had affected her. From that time forward, she was afraid to leave the house. When she did venture out with a member of her family, she had a very hard time speaking to people and making friends. After graduation, she tried several different jobs, but someone always did something to remind her that people were cruel, and so she quit and finally just stayed at home without even trying to live life anymore.

Her parents didn't know what to do with her, so they sought counseling. They wanted their daughter to forget the past and find someone to marry and have a family and life with, but she just continued to withdraw from society. One day when she was twenty-four years old her parents went shopping, and when they returned, they found that she had hung herself in the basement.

Jeff was speechless. Not once had he considered how an event could affect another's life forever. Why hadn't he considered the possible consequences? His mouth hung open and his body turned as a voice from the right said, "Ask for mercy. He is compassionate and waiting for you."

A different voice spoke from the darkness in a low growl, "Do not blame yourself because that girl was weak. You did nothing to her, and you would not have been able to stop your friend from what he did. If you hadn't protected the gang, you would have been blamed too and might have gone to jail. That was self-survival."

"Yes," Jeff thought. "I couldn't have stopped him and they were my friends. Nobody else told the truth either, and the girl didn't even try to go on with her life. I couldn't have done anything else." His defense soothed his mind while God and His laws were not even considered, and the opportunity to say he was sorry and ask for mercy passed by.

The next accusing scene appeared with a swirl of the floor, and this time Jeff had finished college and had just begun working with his Uncle Ben. He was part of management and was treated as a partner in his Uncle's business. Knowing the love that Ben had for him, Jeff took advantage and made certain that he prospered by taking some of the money paid by customers for different jobs and putting it into his pocket. He had done this for a while whenever he thought the funds would not be missed. The actions were acceptable in his mind because he needed the extra money and his Uncle was already wealthy, so taking extra for his salary was alright.

Jeff was completely unaware that his Uncle knew that money was being stolen, and the next view showed his Uncle at church shedding tears in front of the crucifix and praying for the young man he hoped would stop stealing. After a while, Ben's prayers had been answered and the stealing stopped, but Jeff couldn't believe his Uncle had known and had prayed for him. How Ben could possibly have discovered what was happening was unnerving.

The thought of how he had hurt someone who loved him did not touch his heart, but Jeff's only thought was that he could have gotten into trouble. The large amount of love for himself compared to the small amount he had for his Uncle blotted out any caring he should have felt for the man who helped him so much.

The validation process began again. The final verdict in his mind was that he hadn't really hurt anyone. Unfortunately, he did not recognize the grace from above that ended the thefts. A grace from his Uncle's prayers, but Jeff dismissed the incident as something he did and then stopped on his own.

Through all of the confusion he was going through, Jeff still did not accept or believe that forgiveness was necessary and available for all the wrongdoings after the many years of ignoring and offending the Creator. The situation was so overwhelming and his comprehension and knowledge of God so minor, he didn't even consider his faults and the great mercy that was there for the asking. Thoughts that generated were for defending himself only.

The memories did not stop, but the floor rotated again to the next scene and Sarah appeared. Jeff looked at her and knew he still loved her and had hurt her terribly.

"Isn't this the woman you told to get rid of the child you helped to create? See, she holds the child, and it is yours even though she married another." Jeff spun around and saw again the man in black. "See these other women," the man continued. The images of many women he had had an affair with came into view. "The one on the far left conceived from you as well, and she like you didn't want to be tied down or bothered, so she had an abortion. An abortion that you paid for gladly and without remorse."

Jeff began to stutter. He didn't know what to say or what to do about the revelation just presented to him. Sarah had been pregnant and had his baby. That was the baby she had that day he bumped into her and her new husband. He had never known his baby existed and was raised by another.

Knowing that the gruesome tale was true, just a second of honest self-analysis took place. A sudden apprehension came over him that not one time could he remember being really happy or full of joy. Many opportunities had entered his life, but he rejected the feelings of peace and contentment each time the possibility appeared to chase money and material things. Seeing Sarah made that plain. The status and wealth being sought never created happiness, and he knew that all of his life emptiness had lingered within. Instead of pursuing his inner wellbeing and accepting all people, especially those who could have truly changed life, he looked for happiness in material things. He ran after only those things that increased the desolation that was always lurking inside.

True to form, Jeff shook his head and wondered what he was doing. Of course it took two to make a baby, so it certainly was not all his fault. He hadn't known about the child, so what happened hadn't been his choice.

At that instant a voice came into his mind telling the offender that he didn't need to ask for mercy or worry if his sins would never be forgiven and forgotten. He didn't need forgiveness for what he had done because it just didn't matter. At the time, it had been the right thing to do. Besides, loving others had not been important because they would always be there when he decided he wanted them around. It was necessary that he came first.

Unexpectedly, the voice of Emily could be heard. She was talking to someone, and it sounded like they were having a discussion or maybe praying. Maybe it was Fr. Lore. Jeff looked around to see if their conversation made any impact on his surroundings and what he was going through. Both of these people talked to God all of the time, so the hope was that the prayer would help him get back to where they were.

"We will resume," the dark stranger reappeared with eyes snapping. He had also heard the prayers from the hospital room and was outraged at the interference. He added, "Don't forget that we gave you everything you had on earth, and we can continue to give you these pleasurable things." Jeff grasped this weak promise feeling a little hope and believing the master of lies.

The floor began to move and change until he heard laughter. Suddenly, Ralph appeared in front of him. Ralph's kitchen table emerged and he was standing next to the advertiser as they planned how to make the teaching materials and media so cheap, customers would have to come back the next year to purchase again. They both laughed as the discussion turned to high sales and money flowing into their pockets.

Ralph had come up with ideas on how to produce more cheaply, and although Jeff knew the ideas were quite dishonest, he agreed when the advertiser showed him the profit they would be sharing. A second time Jeff stood back a bit from the idea, but his friend told him how most of the kids using the material would never make anything of their lives anyway, so the business owner decided it wouldn't be that dishonest. Kids had to try, and believing most would not, he agreed.

If they charged a little more each year for the same material, they would make that much more. The newer research or the better materials would be much more expensive, and they both knew most schools would not be able to afford it, so higher income schools would be targeted for those. Jeff watched while he sold out to greed.

"Well," he thought, "we just sold the material, so the buyer could have gone somewhere else to purchase the products if they didn't think the instruction fit their needs."

Brett came into view and tried to talk to Jeff about what he was planning to do. The owner dismissed his concerns saying that the business needed to mass produce even if a few of the pages were blurry. Brett had objected, but Jeff insisted that he needed to do that to keep the research going and to make some kind of profit.

The next sight stunned Jeff. He saw Brett talking to his wife in the bedroom of their home. He told his wife that if he didn't do as Jeff asked he would lose his job and not be able to support his family. He went on that his boss was so profit oriented he would never give him a good reference for any other job. Sweat started to flow down Brett's temples as he told his wife that what the owner of the business asked him to do was immoral and would hurt others. Jeff could see the strain this was causing him and wondered if his demands had caused Brett's health problems and finally a stroke.

Why had he not thought his actions through and known that he was hurting the people he loved or should have taken the time to care about? It seemed impossible to him that he had been so utterly insensitive.

The dark figure reappeared, "No, Jeff, the strain put on Brett from your demands did not cause his stroke. He did that himself by thinking the way he did and not trusting that you knew what was best for the organization. It wasn't up to him to tell you what needed to be accomplished; you were the owner and did a good job with the plans and formed a good strategy for the business."

Jeff turned to look at him and decided the man in black was right. He couldn't be responsible for the way people thought or believed allowing themselves to generate constant stress. The stroke was definitely not his fault because he had been good to Brett.

He stopped for a minute and wondered why all of these scenes pointed to him as the bearer of responsibility for everything that happened. The people involved in these instances were adults and could have taken other action if they had wanted to.

Jeff didn't take into account that he had the power and character traits to make or break people who didn't do things his way. No guilt was accepted, and denial ensured no fault fell on the broad shoulders that planned strategies and profits to increase top management income and perks.

The floor seemed to swirl angrily, and the gray atmosphere turned darker still. He saw little children's faces across the nation sitting at desks excited to be learning. There were children of all color and from all levels of society smiling as they waited for their books and manuals to be handed out and their teacher to begin. Many of them were hungry to learn and expand their minds, and only shame was felt by the producer as the students opened their materials and saw how inadequate and hard to read they were.

Jeff saw many children who wanted new materials to absorb, and he knew the manuals they had sent cheated the kids of the opportunity most were looking forward to. The teacher smiled at the children and told them they would use what they could and she would write out more instructions on the blackboard or give a talk to help them understand clearly. But as the teacher turned, he saw a tear come out from the corner of her eye. Jeff thought about his bank book and how it had grown quickly and steadily.

The viewer of his life heard a voice say, "How could these people know that the materials were substandard? What do they have to compare these with? These materials were fine for their purposes."

Jeff's ability to justify was becoming weak. Thinking things through more fully, he finally allowed himself to see that this was a spiritual fight for his soul. Looking to the areas at his right and left, the figures could still be seen, and Jeff contemplated going to the shapes on the right to ask for help. As he took a step that way, he was stopped immediately.

The obnoxious man moved in front of him from the left showing a deep, furrowed brow. His eyes were black as night, and his mouth was turned downward as if it had never seen a smile. When he spoke to Jeff, terrifying and negative vibrations were felt all around. "Are you tired of watching your journey through earthly life? Don't consider asking for their aid; there is nothing they can do. We are coming to the end of the highlights of your life," he stared coldly at Jeff. "Look and continue to watch the fruit you produced!"

The man quickly disappeared, and a woman from the right moved to him and with a very kind smile said, "Pray for mercy."

Jeff opened his mouth to beg for mercy and the man reappeared, "Shut up. You don't want mercy but you do want to go back to your old life.  I can give you that.  You like the things I give like riches and power.  I can allow you to go back to your life and continue earning earthly treasures.  If you decide to change your ways once you are back to your everyday life, you are free to do so."

As he lied to Jeff about his return to physical life, the dying man was trying to reason to himself that he could go back and change the bad he had done.  The shadows on the dark side snickered and laughed softly as Jeff fell for the idea of going back to his earthly life, and he forgot about the kind woman as the thought of a second chance seemed to be the solution.

Emily flashed in front of him, and he saw her asking him to go to Reconciliation.  Jeff had responded that God could wait until he was ready to go.  He was too busy for such things and didn't feel a need to confess anything.  Even though he had been brought up in the church, he had no need for it at this time of his life. God could wait until he had the time and wanted to go back to church.  This was his life not God's and he would do as he pleased.  If he felt the need, he would go to Confession before he died, and he had plenty of time.

Emily had again asked him about making plans for their wedding and he told her to make them.  She could work with Fr. Lore, and he would be there if it fit into his schedule.  Jeff had been uncaring and completely selfish when it came to Emily and hadn't given her any of the love she deserved.

A dark figure appeared in front of the person being reviewed, "Isn't that the woman you offered everything you had and she threw it back at you saying she wasn't interested?  Isn't she the one that you said you would hate forever?"

Jeff turned to look and saw Emily walking out of the restaurant the last night they were together.  His heart began to harden as the rejection that had been felt when she walked out returned and the hatred welled back up in his heart.  His pride refused to let him forget how undeserving she was, and the angry feelings came back. He still hated her for turning him down; the best thing that had ever happened to her. She would never find anyone who could give her the things he could, and so he decided he would depend on his Uncle to pray and help him out of this situation.

"Hatred is good," the odd silhouette said with a smirk. "Continue to hate and never forgive her. She is not at all worthy."

Somehow Jeff felt goaded, but Emily had thrown what he offered back at him. Yes, he was still done with her, so she could stop praying for him. She was a loser and couldn't help him through this. Feeling some satisfaction that this time he was turning away from her, he stood like a statue waiting to see what would be next.

The floor turned different colors, and Jeff saw the hatred he created and kept for Emily looking back at him. Hideous loathing filled his heart until it felt as if it would burst. The scene looking back at him now was something he knew instinctively filled him with a total void. The hatred he created for all of those throughout his life who had hurt, disagreed, or wanted him to change had eaten up everything within and there was nothing left. He caught his breath as he realized what he had done.

Abruptly, he was in church, and he saw people standing in line for Confession. He was not among them and had never asked pardon for any of his sins. A crucifix came into view, and he remembered all he had learned about Christ's horrible death and promise of everlasting life for all who kept faith in Him. Christ asked that all love God and their neighbor. Jeff began to emotionally fall into despair.

He had learned about death from family members and others he had known who had died. As he stared ahead, he could see that throughout his life's journey he had denied the possibility of an early death and chose to believe that he would prepare himself right before it actually happened many, many years into the future. As most people do, he ignored death as something he did not want to think about and chose to live as he pleased instead of making the earthly journey an opportunity to encounter God and become closer to Him. Never did he consider the consequences. How had he gone so long without going to Mass or even thinking about God and all that He had done for Jeff and given to him

"Pray for mercy," the lady on his right said again.

"Who are you?" Jeff asked gently.

"Shut up," the man whirled into sight. "Praying will not help you. Do you want to see more of what you accomplished during your pathetic walk on earth?"

Jeff thought this had been going on for hours, but in fact only minutes had passed by. He was trembling, but he started to pray, "Jesus..."

Before he could continue, the man in black was standing above him with a face that was distorted and looked like a madman's face from the lowest depths of hell. The hatred that spewed from the thing showered Jeff with animosity and was so filled with hostility that the anger of the utterances left marks on his target's face. "Stop trying to make amends. It is too late, and you have been given too many chances. He will not help you or forgive you. Don't you remember His Commandments, but you have spent your entire life loving yourself only. How can you make amends now! It is useless! You ensured your earthly life but wanted nothing to do with your eternal one. He doesn't care about you and never has! We are the ones who helped you all of those years and have given you great pleasure. Stop praying and go to your judgement then return and go back to the life you have known!!!"

All standing around watched to see what the person would do with his last minutes of life. Jeff stood still; so still that not a muscle moved or shifted. Just as he was ready to fall to the ground from fear and anxiety, the atmosphere turned pitch black all around. This shocked him even more, and Jeff could hear others standing in the background. He thought he caught a glimpse of a shadow that was tall and lean. The thing reached towards Jeff, and the man in front of him continued to lie saying, "Get back!!! Do not touch him. We will assist his journey back to earth." The shadow disappeared, but Jeff knew there were others, and they were very close. He didn't understand that the father of deceit was talking to the creature in this manner to ensure Jeff continued with the wrong choice until he stepped over the final threshold.

The scary man turned his attention back to Jeff, "Go to the end of the path and then be judged. You are lost unless you choose what I am offering now. You have no chance of redemption; the life you have lived is plain."

Jeff suddenly heard someone say, "God loves you; ask Him for forgiveness."

Why would God have pity on him now Jeff wondered? Everyone knew his past life, and God would certainly reject him for all of eternity. Asking for forgiveness now would be futile, but he was so desperate he started to pray, "Please Jesus." The powerful man in black screamed "SHUT UP" again so loudly and fiercely that Jeff huddled on the floor.

The frightened man made one more attempt at prayer, "Jesus, please!" The man languishing on the floor had no faith but was grasping for anything that could take this nightmare away. Waiting for a reply, Jeff wondered why He did not speak or appear and take him from this horror. No forgiveness was asked for, and feeling empty inside he decided to accept what he had been told. What the man in black said must be true. Not remembering that belief had to be part of his spiritual world, he was calling to a Savior he had rarely acknowledged throughout his life and was not accepting now. He only wanted to be taken from this terror and put back in his world.

Getting up Jeff continued on, but sorrow still was not shown from the one to be judged. The only emotion he had left was fear of what may be coming. He came to the end of the path and waited to see what would happen next. No more pleading was done, and no attempt to ask for forgiveness was heard. He had no faith in God or hope inside, and the only thought that came to mind was that he wanted the chance to be sent back to try again like the man in black had said.

# CHAPTER TEN

Jeff looked around and saw that he had come to the tree that had watched his progression down the path. He stared at the tree for what seemed to be a long time not understanding what happened to it. From a distance as he had begun his journey down the path, it had looked healthy and beautiful, but now the leaves were either withered or falling off, and the branches were dry and broken. One branch fell off and landed at his feet, so he picked it up and saw that it was full of worms. Dropping it instantly, he turned to move away but stopped quickly. A large figure stood close to him, and as Jeff turned to run, the figure that startled him moved to stop the visitor trying to escape.

Surrounding the beautiful apparition was a stunning purple light that was bright and very intimidating. "I am one of seven who stand before God," he said with a commanding voice to the shaking form in front of him. "Look behind you."

Turning, Jeff's eyes grew big in disbelief as the path he had just taken was completely gone. The maze of plants, trees, and pictures of his life had disappeared. The shadows he had seen along the way on both sides were gone, and there was nothing behind him at all but darkness; a darkness that penetrated through the bones and clutched deep into his heart. He turned quickly back to the vision.

"You are soon to take your last human breath. Earthly life will be over, and the path you traveled on your journey will be ended and will not change once the last breath is gone. You have lost your way as many humans do. Original sin has prompted nothing but selfishness within your spirit, and over time you allowed that greed to spawn disrespect, lawlessness, coveting, great pride, and vanity while vindicating yourself mentally. The few scenes that have just been witnessed are only several that have shaped you until this moment. You have had no faith or hope in God, and your focus is still only on what can be achieved personally. There is no love in your heart for anyone but yourself, and no garment that is suitable to enter into eternal joy surrounds you. Notice the fig tree that was so full of life when you started your journey towards God. Now, the tree is almost dead and crawling with worms. Opportunity to bloom and produce fruit or to assist anyone on their journey has ended. You have been given much. Many graces were bestowed on you during worldly life, and the graces were pushed aside while following foolishness or self-interest that offended God over and over. The great love, protection, and friendship He gave to you every day were dismissed, and all accomplishments and good things were turned into events you told yourself you performed. The choices made were to ignore the real purpose of life, which is growing closer to your Creator, and instead put effort into growing the sin obtained at your conception. You chose to believe that you could decide what was good and what was evil."

Jeff said nothing but looked down. He knew every word the Heavenly being had said was true.

The angel continued, "Your deeds are permanent and will remain held against you unless the alliance to the evil one is ended and the defiance to the Great One turns into a plead for mercy. A change from a hardened heart to an authentic loving heart is required. There is but an instant left for your decision."

As soon as the Heavenly image finished, the dark figure that had accompanied the dying human reappeared. "Do not listen to this ridiculous speaker. He offers you nothing but a boring life in a place that reeks of alliance to a God that did nothing for you. I can provide what you are accustomed to forever. Look at all that I can give," the father of falsehood waved his hand. "There will be no one managing you or any laws that spell out what you must do. You will be FREE!"

Jeff saw a world of material, pleasurable, and status oriented things appear. It was the only world Jeff had accustomed himself to and enjoyed participating in.

"Ask for forgiveness," the lovely apparition said kindly.

"Ask Him for nothing," the dark figure spit out. "He will expect only worship from you, and I will give you everlasting life and happiness. CHOOSE as you always have for comfort and personal pleasure!"

At that moment, Jeff could hear everything that was going on in his hospital room where his body lay. Ben and Emily were praying, and Jeff heard part of Emily's prayer. "At this hour of need oh God, I beg that you forgive Jeff for all of his past discretions. He did go to church and learn about You, but he also followed worldly ways and forgot much of what was taught to him about You. If this is the end of his life, please assist him through his journey to Your judgement so that he chooses You and not the liar who leads so many astray."

Jeff was so distraught he wondered what Emily meant. He had an idea but everything turned into a frightening blur. All he could bring to mind was the way he had lived for so many years.

"Your time is ended," said the magnificent vision who stood by Jeff's side. A fabulous light beam streamed over the dying man, and as he looked at the angel who told him to ask for mercy, then at the darkly dressed figure who offered all of the worldly goods before him and a promise of eternal life with his possessions, and then back at the angel, Jeff chose.............

————————————————————————

Suddenly the two beside Jeff's hospital bed turned to look at him as they heard the alarms begin to go off from the machines that were connected to the vital areas of the physical body.

Emily quickly grasped for Jeff's arm and began to hold his hand. She thought she felt him squeeze her hand for a second but was afraid she was only wishing.

Ben moved to the other side of Jeff's bed in two steps. Emily looked over at him with huge tears in her eyes and said to herself, "Why hadn't Jeff followed more closely in his Uncle's footsteps?"

As they looked at the man lying in front of them, both listened and heard him take his last breath. In the next instant, the machines tracking his vitals showed lines that were flat, and no more beeping noises could be heard. The two looked at each other and began to cry.

Swiftly a nurse came through the door and asked the two visitors to leave. Standing in the corridor, they could hear the nurse call code red, and several doctors hurried down the hallway. They were in the room only a few minutes when Jeff's doctor came out. "I'm sorry, Mr. Bellows is gone."

"Just like that," Ben said. "No warning, no indication. Two days ago Jeff was alive and strong. Now he is gone for good. Why couldn't we have had more time? Why didn't I do more with him and help him more?" He broke down in sobs.

Emily put her arm around him, "You did help him Ben. You spent the time with him he allowed you to. You prayed for him, and you were always there if he needed you. There was nothing else that could have been done. He made his own choices, and it is God who decides when each of us will be called. I pray that Jeff had one last chance to ask God for complete forgiveness and took that opportunity. I know that the Lord would forgive him if he asked, and then when he crossed into the next dimension and faced Jesus, he would be allowed on the one path to glorious eternity. We can hope that he is in

Purgatory or Heaven, and we can continue to pray to God for his soul."

Ben nodded to acknowledge what she had said and then left Emily in the hallway and went back into the room to say goodbye.

www.ingramcontent.com/pod-product-compliance
Lightning Source LLC
Chambersburg PA
CBHW021128020426
42331CB00005B/676